LOL
SPORTS

———— • ————

by

Jack Kreismer

RED-LETTER PRESS, INC.
Saddle River, New Jersey

LOL SPORTS
COPYRIGHT ©2012 Red-Letter Press, Inc.
ISBN-13: 978-1-60387-006-1
ISBN: 1-60387-006-7

Red-Letter Press, Inc.
P.O. Box 393
Saddle River, NJ 07458

www.Red-LetterPress.com

ACKNOWLEDGMENTS

EDITORIAL:
Jeff Kreismer

•

BOOK DESIGN & TYPOGRAPHY:
Jeff Kreismer

•

COVER & CONTENT ART:
Andrew Towl

•

CONTRIBUTORS:
Russ Edwards, Kobus Reyneke, Mike Ryan

Finally, this is to acknowledge that there will be no introduction since we are of the mindset that no one reads them, anyway. At the same time, in keeping with comedy legend Milton Berle's sentiments- "Laughter is an instant vacation"- we wish you a boatload of mini-trips with this LOL book.

–Jack Kreismer, Publisher

Hall of Fame 49ers quarterback Steve Young was poked in the eye during a pileup. He went to the sideline where the trainer recommended he put on an eye patch. Young felt it might hurt his peripheral vision on one side so he refused. Before he went back into the game his coach advised him to rely on the peeper that was okay as he said, "Remember, only the good eye, Young."

A baseball player died and went to Heaven. Once up there, he was able to look down on Hell, where he saw the most spectacular stadium with a capacity crowd, players on the field and a batter at the plate.

"Boy, St. Peter," the ballplayer said. "It looks like a game is just about to start. You call that Hell? I'd love to be playing there."

"That's the hell of it," smiled St. Peter. "So would they, but they don't have a ball."

A snail bought a particularly impressive racecar and decided to enter the Indianapolis 500. To give the car a distinctive look, the snail had a big letter S painted on the hood, sides and trunk before the big event. When the race began, the snail's car immediately took the lead, prompting one of the spectators to say, "Look at that S car go!"

OMG!

After the Rangers lost Game 6 of the 2011 World Series to the Cardinals, Josh Hamilton revealed that God told him he'd hit a home run in the contest. He did, but his team fell short in extra innings. Apparently, Hamilton was not totally surprised. "There was a period at the end (of the sentence). He didn't say you're going to hit it and you're going to win."

• • •

Albert Pujols' wife Deidre said she initially blamed God for an underwhelming contract offer from the St. Louis Cardinals. However, she forgave Him when Pujols received a $254 million deal to play in California. After all, she explained, "It's just like God to put us on a team called the Angels."

• • •

After costing his Bills a victory in 2010 by dropping a wide open touchdown pass, Stevie Johnson blamed God. Tweeted Johnson: "I praise you 24/7!!! And this how you do me!!! You expect me to learn from this??? How??? I'll never forget this!! Ever!!"

WHAT'S THE DIFFERENCE BETWEEN A YANKEE STADIUM AND WRIGLEY FIELD HOT DOG?

Horseplay

A 1989 New Jersey horse race left much to the imagination. With a heavy fog, the announcer could do little to enlighten the spectators: "They race past the stands into the first turn with Hot Lights Excellence in front. On the outside Equal to None is second as they disappear into the fog. From now on...you're on your own!"

Several years later, a Buffalo snowstorm produced a similar call by the track announcer: "Into the far turn...come out...hello... horsies, where are you?"

Nets forward Kris Humphries seemingly makes a peace offering to his estranged partner, Kim Kardashian, as he presents her with a gift. Kim is taken aback and pleasantly surprised. She opens the gift and finds a pair of earrings and a loaded handgun inside. She says, "Thank you so much for these beautiful earrings. My, oh my, this is totally unexpected...but what is this handgun for?"

"That's to pierce your ears."

YOU CAN BUY A YANKEE STADIUM HOT DOG IN OCTOBER.

A Boston marathoner suffered a sudden spell of dizziness so he stopped for a minute and rested his head between his legs.

Seeing this, a preppy Harvard student asked in very proper fashion, "Have you vertigo?"

The marathoner said, "Yes. Four more miles."

What's in a Name?

- A racecar driver was fined $30,000 for losing his composure and making an obscene gesture. His name? Will Power.

- In 2011, the St. John's Red Storm recruited the son of a Nigerian minister to play on their basketball team. His name? God's Gift Achiuwa. His brother's name? God's Will.

- When 7'2" Dikembe Mutombo, a four time NBA defensive player of the year, was born in Zaire on June 25, 1966, he was named Dikembe Mutombo Mpolondo Mukamba Jean-Jacque Wamutombo.

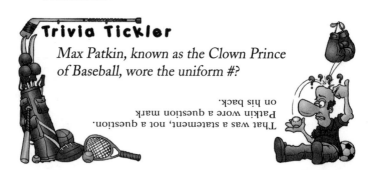

Trivia Tickler

Max Patkin, known as the Clown Prince of Baseball, wore the uniform #?

That was a statement, not a question. Patkin wore a question mark on his back.

- Horse racing legend Man O' War suffered his only defeat in 20 races- to a horse named Upset.

- Shortly after Laker Ron Artest changed his name to Metta World Peace, actor Albert Brooks remarked on Twitter, "(L.A.) Dodgers file for bankruptcy. (Owner) Frank McCourt changes name to Metta World Bank."

A sports nut was strolling along the Cleveland shores of Lake Erie when he spotted a bottle floating in the water. As it drifted ashore, he picked it up and out popped a Genie.

"Master, Master," said the Genie, I am eternally grateful that you have released me from my bondage in this bottle. It has been ages since I've experienced freedom. For your reward, ask any three wishes and I will grant them to you."

The guy thought for a moment and said, "I would like for three things to happen this year- for the Indians to win the World Series, the Cavs to win the NBA title, and the Browns to win the Super Bowl."

The Genie pondered this for a second- and then jumped back in the bottle.

Before he had his liposuction, Jets coach Rex Ryan was so heavy that when he stepped on the digital scale it said, "To be continued."

A guy had been stranded on an island for ages. One day as he was walking on the beach, a beautiful woman in a wet suit emerged from the surf. "Hey, cutie pie. Have you been here long?" she asked.

"I reckon about ten years."

"Do you smoke?"

"Oh, what I'd do for a cigarette!" he moaned.

With that, she unzipped a pocket in the sleeve of her wet suit, pulled out a pack of cigarettes, lit one and gave it to him. "I guess it's been a long while since you've had a drink, huh?"

"You got that right," he said.

She pulled out a flask from another pocket, gave it to him and he anxiously took a long, hard swig. I bet you haven't played around in a while either," she cooed as she began to unzip the front of her wet suit.

Positively wide-eyed with anticipation, he gasped, "Don't tell me you have a set of golf clubs in there too?"

QUOTE, UNQUOTE

Sports Horoscope

Aquarius (Jan 20-Feb 18) The Office Pool
Born under the sign of the office pool, you can soon expect to
pick up a bundle at the track. Just be sure to spread it around the
rose bushes as soon as possible.

Pisces (Feb 19-Mar 20) The Protective Cup
The conjunction of Mars and Jupiter will bring you the "Most
Valuable Player" award after the big game. Unfortunately, it'll be
from your poker buddies.

Aries (Mar 21-Apr 19) The Beer Belly
All your friends consider you the biggest sports fan they know.
That's because when it comes to blowing a lot of hot air around,
you da' man!

Taurus (Apr 20-May 20) The Armchair Quarterback
The stars say you can expect to be on the cover of *Sports
Illustrated.* Someone will leave it on the bench just before
you sit down.

Gemini (May 21-Jun 21) The Ref
The transit of Neptune means that you're not all that athletic.
Most guys stay in shape by pumping iron. Your idea of staying in
shape is pumping gas.

Cancer (Jun 22-Jul 22) The Jock
Your softball skills will earn you much fame. You'll be invited to
Times Square next New Year's Eve for a special honor...They'll
want you to drop the ball.

Leo (Jul 23-Aug 22) The Sports Bar
You spend so much time watching baseball, you actually believe that the last words to the national anthem are "Play Ball!"

Virgo (Aug 23-Sep 22) The Season Pass
Your talents will lead you to develop a new workout program for sports fans—"Beer-oebics"—zip, lift, chug, crunch, zip, lift, chug, crunch...

Libra (Sep 23-Oct 23) The Catcher's Mitt
You possess the physique of a champion skier... going downhill fast.

Scorpio (Oct 24-Nov 21) The Bench
When it comes to football, you'll play in the Ivy League. After every game, you'll wind up attached to an I-V.

Sagittarius (Nov 22-Dec 21) The Six Pack
Soon, your appearance on the field will hearten and inspire the entire team...too bad it's the opposing team.

Capricorn (Dec 22-Jan 19) The Groin Pull
The stars portend that you will some day be the starting pitcher for the New York Yankees. Of course, that will only be when the regular water boy is late.

A Wonder Boy and His Dog

It wasn't just Tim Tebow who had to make a big move from Denver to New York when he was dealt to the Jets. The QB brought with him his Rhodesian ridgeback, Bronco. However, realizing that his pooch's name didn't exactly fit in with his new surroundings, Tebow got creative. His pet now goes by "Bronx."

Hot Corner Potato

In a 1980s minor league baseball game, Williamsport hosted
Reading. With an act that could've been drawn up in the
schoolyard, perhaps it was fitting that the game's memorable
moment occurred in the same city as the Little League World
Series. With a Reading runner on third, Williamsport catcher
Dave Bresnahan had a trick up his sleeve. Actually, it was in his
catcher's mitt. There, Bresnahan kept a potato hidden. After a
pitch, he grabbed the potato and purposely threw it wildly toward
third base. The runner, believing it was the baseball, trotted
home. When he arrived there, Bresnahan greeted him with the
baseball he was still holding. However, the umpire, not amused,
called the runner safe. Neither were Bresnahan's bosses. The next
day, he was let go.

The challenger was getting clobbered by the heavyweight champ.
After the first round he stumbled back to his corner where his
trainer said, "Let him hit you with left hooks in the second. Your
face is crooked."

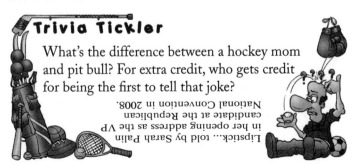

Trivia Tickler

What's the difference between a hockey mom
and pit bull? For extra credit, who gets credit
for being the first to tell that joke?

Lipstick… told by Sarah Palin
in her opening address as the VP
candidate at the Republican
National Convention in 2008.

Off The Wall

SIAMESE TWINS LOVE DOUBLEHEADERS

GOLFERS ARE BEST WHEN THEY'RE NOT UP TO PAR

ATHLETE'S FOOT COMES FROM ATHLETE'S FEAT

OLD BOWLING BALLS WIND UP IN THE GUTTER

YOU CAN'T PLAY TENNIS WITHOUT RAISING A RACKET

BASKETBALL PLAYERS TELL TALL TALES

A TIMEKEEPER IS A CLOCK-EYED MAN

OLD QUARTERBACKS NEVER DIE... THEY JUST PASS AWAY

TENNIS PLAYERS HAVE A LOT OF FAULTS

WHAT'S KEVIN DURANT'S
FAVORITE PLACE TO EAT?

Muggsy and Buggsy had been together in Hell for many, many years. Their eternal job was to shovel coal into the fires side by side. Suddenly, one day they felt cold air. The air got colder and colder. Snow began to fall. The next thing they knew, there was a blizzard. The snow blanketed the ground and extinguished the fires. Next, a gust of frigid wind froze over the entire surface of Hell!

"What the heck is going on here?" Muggsy wondered out loud.

Buggsy answered, "I don't know for sure, Muggsy, but I have a hunch that the Bills just won the Super Bowl."

Bobo the Gorilla was making a fortune for his owner. They'd travel around to golf courses and challenge the pro to a round of golf. The hot-shots always accepted the bet, figuring that they could easily beat the muscle-bound primate. That was, until Bobo stepped up to the tee and drove the ball 450 yards. Then they'd usually give up, pay the bet and scamper away to find solace at the Nineteenth Hole. One morning, a top-rated country club pro conceded the bet after the gorilla drove the ball 450 yards to the green. "Just out of curiosity," the pro asked as he forked over the cash, "how does Bobo putt?"

"The same as he drives," said the gorilla's owner. "450 yards."

DUNKIN' DONUTS

Banking It In

In a Twitter image posted by DeShawn Stevenson, the Nets guard revealed an ATM in his kitchen. Perhaps it shouldn't come as a surprise considering he has a tattoo of the man adorning the $5 bill, Abraham Lincoln, on his neck. According to USA Today, Stevenson has earned over $25 million from his NBA salary over the past decade. With his new machine, he will have now cash at his disposal faster than you can say, "Show me the money."

Two runners were trailing the pack in the marathon. The guy who was second-to-last was poking fun at the runner behind him. "Hey, how does it feel to be last?"

"Well, if you must know," said the other guy... And then he dropped out.

Three guys desperately want to get into the Olympic stadium but the Games are sold out so they decide to pose as athletes. The first guy picks up a long piece of pipe, walks up to the athletes' entrance and says to the guard, "I'm a pole vaulter." The guard lets him in.

The second guy appears with a manhole cover and says, "Discus thrower." He's also allowed in.

The third guy shows up carrying a roll of barbed wire. Confused, the guard looks up and the guy says, "fencing."

We Can't Make This Stuff Up...

In 2007, Gabe Gross of the Milwaukee Brewers was thrown out at third after manager Ned Yost's scratch of a mosquito bite was misinterpreted for a steal sign... Former horse racing Triple Crown winner Affirmed once got loose at Hollywood Park, prompting a trackwide search. The missing horse was located back in his own stall - which he had found among 2,244 others... In 1916, Cumberland College gained three yards on the first play of the game against Georgia Tech. It was all downhill after that, as they suffered the worst football defeat in college history, 222-0... Jack Dempsey bought a Rolls-Royce after each successful heavyweight title fight - six in all... A member of Tokyo's 2016 Olympic bid committee, fearing the perils of global warming, warned that, "It could be that the 2016 Games are the last Olympics in the history of mankind"... The winner of the 1898 Boston Marathon was Ronald McDonald.

QUOTE, UNQUOTE

No comment.

-Michael Jordan, on being named
to the NBA All-Interview Team

A guy was nodding off in his recliner when his wife sneaks up and whacks him on the noggin with a frying pan. Startled, the guy shakes off his cobwebs and says, "What was that for?"

"That was for the piece of paper in your shirt pocket with the name Kelly Ann written on it."

"Aw, shucks," he explains, "a couple of weeks ago when I went to the races, Kelly Ann was one of the horses I bet on."

The wife apologizes for the misunderstanding. A week later, the husband is reading the paper in his favorite chair when she hits him with an even bigger frying pan and knocks him out cold. When he regains his senses, he says, "Geez, what was that for?"

"Your horse called."

Two guys were at the ol' fishing hole when one says to the other, "I love bein' out here, whiling away the hours, takin' a sip and waitin' for a bite- the solitude, the fresh air. Say, why do you fish?"

"My son's taking trumpet lessons."

Trivia Tickler

Who ran the bases backwards in 1963 to celebrate his 100th career home run?

Jimmy Piersall of the New York Mets

Little Johnny was in his kindergarten class when the teacher asked the kids what their dads did for a living. The usual jobs came up- fireman, salesman, policeman. Johnny, however was uncharacteristically shy about giving an answer. Finally, the teacher said, "Johnny, how about you? What does your father do for a living?"

Johnny murmured, "My dad's an exotic dancer."

The startled teacher quickly ended that segment of class and sent the other kids off to do some coloring. Then she took little Johnny aside and said, "Is that really true about your father?"

"No," said Johnny, "he plays for the Cubs but I was too embarrassed to say it."

Derby Downer

The 1957 Kentucky Derby saw one of the biggest blunders in horseracing history. English-bred Gallant Man, jockeyed by the legendary Willie Shoemaker, held a comfortable lead nearing the homestretch. Shoemaker, however, mistook the 16th pole for the finish line and momentarily stood up in his saddle. His unfortunate action allowed jockey Willie Hartack and his horse, Iron Liege, to close the gap and overtake Gallant Man. While Shoemaker quickly resumed driving his mount, Gallant Man was unable to catch Iron Liege. He lost by a nose.

Before the race, Gallant Man owner Ralph Lowe told the Churchill Downs track superintendents about a dream he had the previous night. Lowe explained how his jockey "stood up in the stirrups" on the colt. Sure enough, that nightmare became reality.

Court Jesters

"If you really want to enjoy sports, do what I did. Become a Harlem Globetrotters fan. There's no losing, no stats, no strikes, no trades, no contract hassles, no postseason, and no annoying media. Just winning, all the time, every night. By the way, I'm just diseased enough to realize it would also be fun to root for the Washington Generals, the team that loses to the Globetrotters every night. At least you wouldn't have to put up with all that annoying, preseason optimism." -George Carlin

• • •

In a 1974 contest, Lakers center Elmore Smith stood at the foul line with three shots ahead of him. He needed to make only two to keep the game going. Not only did Smith miss all three- on each one of his shots he came up with nothing but air.

• • •

Wake Forest baseball coach Tom Walter wanted to give a gift to one of his players, but had to make sure with the NCAA that his gesture didn't qualify as an "extra benefit." When associate athletic director Todd Hairston gave him the thumbs up, Walter donated his kidney to freshman Kevin Jordan.

QUOTE, UNQUOTE

What impressed me most is that Webb's time was a full two seconds faster than Barry Bonds' home-run trot.

-Scott Osler, after Allan Webb ran
the mile in a record of 3:53:43

It's only fitting that on a day of remembrance, Metta World Peace forgot. On May 28, 2012, the artist formerly known as Ron Artest tweeted "Happy labor day... Enjoy it." After realizing his mistake, he later deleted the post and corrected himself.

• • •

When told he was misquoted in his own autobiography, Hall of Famer Charles Barkley said, "I should have read it."

• • •

Bill Russell had an impersonator who was almost a dead ringer for the basketball Hall of Famer except for one thing: he was nine inches shorter than the 6'9" Celtics former center. The Russell wannabe got around this by claiming he had shortening surgery so he could fit into his Mercedes.

• • •

With an NBA Lockout looming, Deron Williams signed with the Turkish Basketball League during the 2011 offseason. While his time there was short, he clearly made an impression. His Besiktas team retired his #8 jersey after only 15 games.

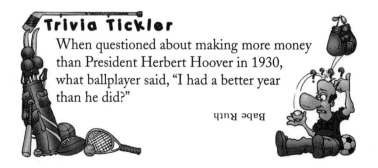

Trivia Tickler

When questioned about making more money than President Herbert Hoover in 1930, what ballplayer said, "I had a better year than he did?"

Babe Ruth

Beethoven's Ninth Symphony was being performed at the famed Carnegie Hall. During intermission, the conductor becomes frantic when he realizes the last few pages of his sheet music are missing. After telling his assistant this, the trusted aide remembers that the missing pages were accidentally locked in the dressing room. He assures the conductor that they'll be on his music stand in time for when they are needed.

"I would hope so," growls the conductor. "And while you're at it, keep an eye on the bass players. They've been drinking ever since the intermission started."

The conductor then goes about his business while the assistant makes sure the bass players down a few cups of coffee before they return to their orchestra seats.

As the curtain rises for the remainder of the symphony, the assistant rushes to find a security guard to open the dressing room. He finds one and hurries him down to the locked room.

"What's all the fuss about?" asks the security guard.

The assistant replies, "It's the bottom of the ninth, the score is tied, and the bassists are loaded!"

WHAT'S THE DIFFERENCE BETWEEN A FOOTBALL AND PRINCE CHARLES?

A miserable, no-good golfer goes to Hell. His eternal punishment is to serve as a caddie for the devil. This is not your normal golf bag toting duty. The devil plays with a hot hand...oven-heated golf clubs and balls. Just as the guy is prepared to caddie for the first time in Hell, he sees a former playing partner, a hideously ugly man, on the first tee with a beautiful woman. The eternally damned caddie mutters out loud, "Why do I have to suffer like this when that guy gets to spend his time with a gorgeous woman like that?"

The devil hears him and says, "Who do you think you are to question that woman's punishment?"

Bird's the Word

While it's not all that unusual for a baseball card to be printed with an error, there was one instance in particular in which the manufacturer was understandably embarrassed. The card was a 1989 Fleer Billy Ripken. Pictured in his Baltimore Orioles uniform, Ripken's bat was perched over his right shoulder with the bottom of the knob visible. The original version was printed with an expletive that had been written on the knob. When the error was found, Fleer rushed to correct it, resulting in variations of the card being covered with marker, brushed with whiteout, and airbrushed. Needless to say, the uncensored card remains the most sought after version.

ONE'S THROWN TO THE AIR, THE OTHER
HEIR TO THE THRONE

A guy from San Francisco, a guy from Detroit and a guy from Seattle are granted a talk with God. They're each allowed one question. The guy from San Francisco inquires, "Will there ever be a time when we don't have to worry about earthquakes?"

God responds, "Yes, but not in your lifetime."

Then the guy from Detroit asks, "God, will there ever be a time when our city has no crime?"

Again God replies, "Yes, but not in your lifetime."

Finally, the guy from Seattle asks, "God, will the Mariners ever win the World Series?"

God answers, "Yes, but not in my lifetime!"

A Jewish football player received a scholarship to Notre Dame. When there was a semester break, he flew home. His rabbi bumped into him at the airport. Aware that the player was a member of the Fighting Irish football team the rabbi said, "Tell me, son. They haven't converted you to their ways, have they?"

The football star answered, "Why, no ... absolutely not, Father!"

Then there was the dentist who complimented the hockey player on his nice, even teeth: one, three, five, seven and nine were missing.

There Is No Joy In Friendsville

From 1967 to 1973, Tennessee's Friendsville Academy high school basketball team chalked up a national record 138 consecutive losses. They lost one game 71 to 0 but another only 2 to 0 when the winning basket was scored by a Friendsville player, who shot the ball into the wrong hoop.

In 1970, the coach named one player--a player who had never scored a single point--the team's MVP. When reporter Douglas S. Looney from the National Observer questioned the coach, he tersely replied, "You don't think scoring is everything, do you?"

The conversation continued with the reporter asking, "Is there anything this team does well?"

"Not really," replied the coach.

"Are you making progress?"

"I couldn't truthfully say that we are."

"Do you like coaching?"

"I don't care that much for basketball."

QUOTE, UNQUOTE

Bob Gibson is the luckiest pitcher I ever saw. He always pitches when the other team doesn't score any runs.

-Tim McCarver, on the Hall of Famer

Bottoms Up!

• Comedian Roseanne Barr and former hubby Tom Arnold mooned the crowd at the Oakland Coliseum during a 1989 A's-Giants World Series game, revealing cheeky "Rosie" and "Tom" tattoos, respectively.

• Red Sox pitcher Clarence Blethen, who carried his false teeth in his back pocket, only reached base once in his big league career. When he went to slide into second, his teeth bit him in the rear, forcing him to come out of the game due to excessive bleeding.

• In 1961 at Wimbledon, American tennis player Pat Stewart had her phone number embroidered on her panties.

• The world ranked beach volleyball pair of Zara Dampney and Shauna Mullin inked a deal to wear bikini bottoms bearing a bar code- one that, when photographed by a smartphone, takes you to the gambling site Betfair.com.

• 26-yard old Mark Harvey stormed the field wearing Batman's cape and underwear during the Baltimore Orioles home opener in 2012. As a result, the caped crime fighter has been banned from Camden Yards for life by the club.

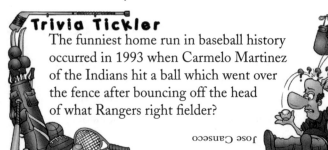

Trivia Tickler

The funniest home run in baseball history occurred in 1993 when Carmelo Martinez of the Indians hit a ball which went over the fence after bouncing off the head of what Rangers right fielder?

Jose Canseco

A guy comes home from work, plops himself onto his Barcolounger in the family room, grabs the remote, and flips on the football game on the big screen HDTV. He yells into the kitchen, "Honey, bring me a cold one before it starts."

His wife brings him a chilled mug of beer. A few minutes later, he calls out to the wife again, "Honey, bring me another beer before it starts."

Again, his wife brings him a beer. A short time later, he yells a third time, "Honey, hurry up and bring me another beer before it starts."

The wife, now exasperated, marches into the family room and says, "You bum. I've been doing the wash... the dishes... the ironing... and now I'm waiting on you hand and foot!"

As she reads him the riot act, the husband rolls his eyes and sighs quietly, "Oh no, it's started already."

Dallas Cowboys owner Jerry Jones, accompanied by some media types, struts into an old folks' home to mingle with the people and pick up some good p.r. at the same time. He walks up to a sweet little old lady in a wheelchair who smiles at him with an otherwise blank stare.

"Do you know who I am?" says Jones.

She responds, "No, but if you ask at the desk, they'll tell you."

One day during recess, the new elementary school teacher, Mrs. Jones, noticed that little Johnny was all by himself on one side of the playground while all the other kids were playing soccer at the other end. Mrs. Jones asked Johnny if something was bothering him. Johnny said, "There aint nuthin' bothering me, ma'am."

A bit later, Mrs. Jones noticed that Johnny was in the same spot, again, all by his lonesome. She went up to him and said, "Would you like me to be your friend?"

Johnny eyed her suspiciously, then said, "Well, I guess so."

Now Mrs. Jones felt she was making some headway so she asked, "Why are you standing here all by yourself?"

"Because," Johnny said with a good deal of frustration, "I'm the damn goalie!"

A couple of guys were sitting behind two nuns at a Red Sox game at Fenway. The nuns were dressed in habits and the guys were having a tough time seeing over their tops. At one point, they decided to antagonize the nuns to get them to move. One guy loudly says to the other, "I think I'd like to move to Texas. I hear there are very few Catholics there."

The other guy, speaking loudly enough for the nuns to hear, says, "I hear there are even fewer Catholics in Georgia. I certainly wouldn't mind going there."

One of the nuns turns around and matter-of-factly says, "Why don't you go to Hell? There aren't any Catholics there."

Tennis Lobs

Q: Why shouldn't you fall for a tennis player?
A: To them, love means nothing.

Q: Where does a tennis player go for entertainment?
A: Volley-wood

Q: How do you know if you're really cross-eyed?
A: You can watch a tennis match without moving your head.

• • •

Two cats are sitting on a wall, watching a tennis match. One says to the other, "Why are you interested in this stuff?"

The other says, "My dad's in the racket."

• • •

How many tennis players does it take to screw in a light bulb?

"What do you mean it was out? It was in!!"

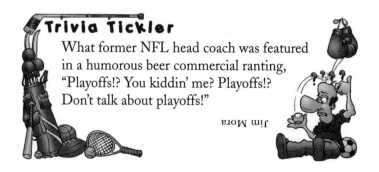

Trivia Tickler

What former NFL head coach was featured in a humorous beer commercial ranting, "Playoffs!? You kiddin' me? Playoffs!? Don't talk about playoffs!"

Jim Mora

Then there was the Russian tennis player whose game was great at the nyet.

• • •

"The way a man plays tennis can be very revealing. I was playing tennis with a man I had been dating for a while and noticed his reluctance to keep score properly. He couldn't say, 'Thirty-love.' He kept saying, 'Thirty, I really like you but still have to see other people.'" -Rita Rudner

Amazing Appeal

In their inaugural year, the 1962 New York Mets set a mark for the worst won-loss record in baseball history, 40-120. One incident in one game typified their futility. The "Amazing" Mets were playing the Chicago Cubs at the Polo Grounds. "Marvelous" Marv Throneberry had just slammed a two-run triple and was standing on third when Chicago first baseman Ernie Banks called for the ball to appeal that Marv had missed first base. The appeal was upheld and Throneberry was called out. Mets manager Casey Stengel ran out from the dugout to argue the call only to be waved off by veteran umpire Dusty Boggess who said, "Forget it, Casey. He didn't touch second either!"

WHY IS IT DIFFICULT TO DRIVE A GOLF BALL?

A husband and wife, both golf fanatics, were discussing the future as they sat by a warm fireplace. "Dear," the wife said, "if I died, would you remarry?"

The husband responded, "Well, if something were to happen to you in the near future, I guess so. After all, we're not exactly senior citizens."

"Would you live in this house with her?" the wife asked.

"I would think so."

She continued, "How about my car? Would she get that?"

"I don't see why not."

"What about my golf clubs? Would you give them to her too?"

"Oh, goodness gracious no, never," the husband exclaimed. "She's left-handed."

Did you hear about the short music afficionado
who tried out for the Olympics?
He's a compact disc thrower.

BECAUSE IT DOESN'T
HAVE A STEERING WHEEL

The Babe's Greatest Hit

Babe Ruth may get the credit he deserves as a baseball player, but not his due as a practical joker. Bill Werber, Ruth's Yankee teammate, recounts perhaps the Bambino's most polarizing prank.

Ruth's victim was Ed Wells, a former Tigers pitcher who joined the Yanks in 1929. Following a game in Detroit, Ruth had Wells join him for a double date that evening. He told Wells that the girls loved to drink and that Wells was to supply a fifth of gin while Ruth bought a bag of oranges for a mix.

When they arrived at the suburban home, it wasn't the two ladies who greeted them at the door. Rather, it was a furious man, who yelled, "So you're the scum who's been after my wife. I oughtta kill ya!" With that, the man pulled out a snub-nosed pistol and fired at Ruth.

"I'm hit Ed!" Babe screamed, collapsing onto the porch. "Run, run for your life!" Wells bolted from the scene, fully expecting not to make it out alive. Nevertheless, he managed to make it all the way back to the Book Cadillac Hotel where the Yankees were staying on their road trip.

QUOTE, UNQUOTE

I still love Don, he's a great guy.
But he's evil, and he steals people's money.

-Mike Tyson, in 1999, on
boxing promoter Don King

At the hotel, he was greeted by grim-faced teammates in the lobby. Tony Lazzeri told Wells, "Babe's been shot. He's in bad shape and has been asking for you."

Wells was taken to Ruth's room, where the Babe was laid out in bed with talcum powder covering his face and ketchup adorning his white shirt. "He's dying, Ed," Earl Combs sobbed.

Wells passed out on the scene, but the thunder of laughter that followed quickly revived him. According to Werber, "even later we never could persuade Ed of the humor in the situation."

At a hoity-toity country club where rules of golf are strictly enforced, a member saw a guest of the club place his ball five inches in front of the tee markers. The member hurriedly went over to the guest and said, "Sir, I don't know whether you've ever played here before, but we have very stringent rules about placing your tee at or behind the markers before driving the ball."

The guest looked the snooty club member right in the eye and retorted, "First, I've never played here before. Second, I don't care about your rules. And third, this is my second shot."

Maybe you've heard about the jockey who was a tremendous overeater. He kept putting a la carte before the horse.

Three punch-drunk fighters go for a psychological evaluation. The psychiatrist says to the first one, "How much is three times three?"

The fighter thinks for a moment and says, "Wednesday."

The psychiatrist shakes his head and says to the second fighter, "How much is three times three?"

The second fighter answers, "273."

The psychiatrist shakes his head sadly and says to the third, "Can you tell me what is three times three?"

The third fighter says, "Sure- nine."

"Excellent!" says the psychiatrist. "And how did you arrive at that?"

"Simple... I subtracted 273 from Wednesday."

The turtles and skunks decide to have a soccer match. The turtles' team is slow as molasses while the skunks' team just plain stinks. The game is scoreless with just seconds to go when, suddenly, a centipede—picked up as a ringer by the skunks— rushes onto the field, gets a pass, dribbles the ball, shoots and scores as the shell-shocked turtles watch the game go by the boards.

Afterwards, the coach of the skunks asks the centipede, "Where have you been all game?"

The centipede answers, "I was stringing up my cleats."

Turning Red

In the middle of a 2004 Brazilian soccer match, a referee reached into his pocket to pull out a red card to eject a player. Instead, he pulled out a pair of red panties. With a face to match the dainties, the ref said he had no idea how the undergarment got there, but was so embarrassed that he called off the rest of the game.

Terrell Owens, Tom Brady and Jerry Rice are standing before God at the Pearly Gates. The Lord looks at them and says, "Before I grant you a place at my side, I must first ask you what you believe in." He asks Brady, "What is it that you believe?"

The Patriots quarterback looks at God and says with great passion, "I've been a Super Bowl winner more than once and I believe I have brought great joy to the fans of New England as a result. I believe in good sportsmanship on the field at all times and I think I've done that. More importantly, I believe one needs a strong sense of morals and values off the field and I would hope you think I've exhibited that, God."

QUOTE, UNQUOTE

I don't know. I've never played there.

-Sandy Lyle, golfer, when asked his opinion
of Tiger Woods in 1992

"That I do, Mr. Brady. Take the seat to my left...And you, Mr. Rice?"

"Well, Lord, you know all things. You're well aware of my Hall of Fame career; of the many records I set, primarily due to the fact I always kept in the greatest shape possible. Indeed, I believe in keeping the body and mind as sound as possible."

"That you've done, Mr. Rice. I'm proud of you. You may take the seat to my right...And you, Mr. Owens. What do you believe?"

"I believe you're in my seat."

Foul Territory

What's worse than having your gold tooth fall into a toilet at Citi Field during a Mets game? Going in after it and having your arm stuck for hours as the high vacuum system continuously tries to flush you. A female Mets fan got into just that predicament, doing about as well in the john as the Mets were on the field. The plumber who installed the system had to be located and he finally managed to extract her after several hours of being flushed up to her armpit. She lost her tooth and the Mets lost the game- so ends the story in Flushing, New York.

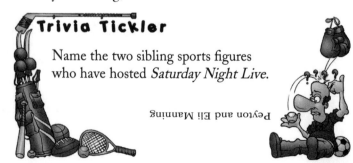

Trivia Tickler

Name the two sibling sports figures who have hosted *Saturday Night Live*.

Peyton and Eli Manning

The Blunderful Broadcaster

After his Major League playing career, Jerry Coleman became even more well-known for his malaprops as the long-time play-by-play man of the Padres. Here's some of his "finest" work.

• *Hi folks, I'm Johnny Grubb. No I'm not. This is Jerry Coleman.*

• *Benedict may not be hurt as much as he really is.*

• *He (Graig Nettles) leaped up to make one of those diving stops only he can make.*

• *Ozzie Smith just made another play that I've never seen anyone else make before, and I've seen him make it more than anyone else ever has.*

• *Winfield goes back to the wall, he hits his head on the wall and it rolls off! It's rolling all the way back to second base. This is a terrible thing for the Padres.*

• *And Kansas City is at Chicago tonight, or is that Chicago at Kansas City? Well, no matter, Kansas City leads in the eighth, four to four.*

• *There's somebody warming up in the bullpen, but he's obscured by his number.*

• *Next up is Fernando Gonzalez, who is not playing tonight.*

• *Rich Folkers is throwing up in the bullpen.*

• *There's a hard shot to LeMaster, and he throws Madlock into the dugout.*

• *McCovey swings and misses, and it's fouled back.*

• *Larry Lintz steals second standing up. He slid, but he didn't have to.*

• *The new Haitian baseball can't weigh more than four ounces or less than five.*

• *The ex-left-hander Dave Roberts will be going for Houston.*

• *Hector Torrez, how can you communicate with Enzo Hernandez when he speaks Spanish and you speak Mexican?*

• *Billy Almon has all of his inlaw and outlaws here this afternoon.*

• *Sometimes, big trees grow out of acorns. I think I heard that from a squirrel.*

• *The Phillies beat the Cubs today in the doubleheader. That puts another keg in the Cubs' coffin.*

• *If (Pete) Rose's streak were still intact, with that single to left, the fans would be throwing babies out of the upper deck.*

• *I've made a couple of mistakes I'd like to do over.*

WHAT DO THE CHARLOTTE BOBCATS AND POSSUMS HAVE IN COMMON?

Four old duffers had a Saturday morning 8 o'clock tee time for years. On one such morning, they noticed a guy watching them as they teed off. At every tee, he caught up with them and had to wait.

When they reached the fifth tee, the guy walked up to the foursome and handed them a card which read, "I am deaf and mute. May I play through?" The old duffers were outraged and signaled to him that nobody plays through their group. He'd just have to bide his time.

On the eighth hole, one of the foursome was in the fairway lining up his second shot. All of the sudden he got bopped in the back of the head by the stinging force of a golf ball. He turned around and looked back at the tee angrily. There stood the deaf mute, frantically waving his arm in the air, holding up four fingers.

"Do you have any green golf balls here?" the duffer asks the sporting goods sales guy.

"You might find them at a miniature golf course, but you're not gonna find 'em here... Why would you want green golf balls, anyway?"

"They're easier to find in the sand trap."

BOTH PLAY DEAD AT HOME
AND GET KILLED ON THE ROAD.

A Jets fan, Giants fan and Cowboys fan traveled to Saudi Arabia where they shared a smuggled case of vodka, an illegal activity punishable by death! The Saudi police got wind of the offense and arrested them. Fortunately, the fans had some very good lawyers and were able to reduce the ultimate punishment to life in prison.

As luck would have it, on the day their trial ended, it was the birthday of the Sheik's wife, a Saudi national holiday. The Sheik was feeling particularly benevolent on this celebratory occasion so he decided that they could be set free after only receiving ten lashes each of the whip. In honor of his wife's birthday, the Sheik further declared, "I am going to allow you each one wish before your whipping is administered."

The Jets fan thought quickly and said, "I would like a pillow tied behind my back." His wish was granted and made the whiplashing practically painless.

Next up, was the Giants fan. For his single wish, he asked that two pillows be tied behind his back. That said and done, his lashing was barely felt.

Finally, it was the Cowboys fan turn to be whipped. "And what is your one wish before you receive your thrashing?" the Sheik asked the Cowboys fan.

"Please tie the Giants fan to my back."

Q: Why were the Nets the last NBA team to get a website?
A: Because they couldn't put up three W's in a row.

Spellbinding

• The Minnesota Timberwolves handed out posters with their nickname spelled W-O-V-E-S on "Reading to Succeed Night" at the Target Center in Minneapolis.

• During a World Series broadcast, network commentator Tim McCarver proclaimed, "It's a five-letter word- S-T-R-I-K-E."

• In the mid 1970s at Florida's Derby Lane greyhound track, one of the dogs was named Cilohocla. The origin of the dog's name remained a mystery until someone thought to reverse the spelling.

• An Ohio State online photo gallery depicted Buckeyes fans spelling out O-H-I-O with their bodies. It featured a shot in which the corpse of a man in a coffin played the role of the I.

• A student at Elgin, Illinois, high school had to remove a Cubs shirt she was wearing because an authority thought FUKUDOME was a curse word.

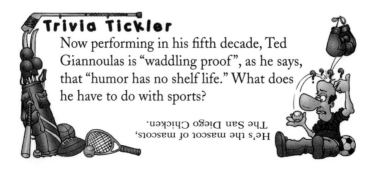

Trivia Tickler

Now performing in his fifth decade, Ted Giannoulas is "waddling proof", as he says, that "humor has no shelf life." What does he have to do with sports?

He's the mascot of mascots, The San Diego Chicken.

• In 1995, Notre Dame football fan Dan O'Connor decided to have the Fighting Irish slogan imprinted tattooed on his arm. The tattoo artist left O'Connor's wallet $125 light and his arm one-letter short. The moniker was plastered "**Fighing** Irish."

• Following his first national championship, Kentucky basketball coach John Calipari received many local honors. One of them was in Pikeville, KY, where he received a ceremonial key to the city, attached to an engraved plaque. The plaque read: "To Coach John Calipari In Recognition Of A Remarkable Season And Returning **Th** NCAA National Championship Trophy To The Commonwealth Of Kentucky. **It's** Rightful Home."

• In 1960, the Chicago White Sox became the first big league team to put player names on the backs of uniforms- and also the first to do so incorrectly. On a road trip to New York, the back of first baseman Ted Kluszewski 's jersey featured a backwards "z" and an "x" instead of "k" in his name.

• In a game against the Marlins in 2009, Adam Dunn and Ryan Zimmerman, two of the top hitters on the Washington Nationals, were sent onto the field wearing "Natinals" jerseys.

QUOTE, UNQUOTE

That is really a lovely horse.
I once rode her mother.

-Ted Walsh, horse racing commentator

At one point during a baseball game, little Johnny's coach called him over. "Do you understand what team play is?" asked the coach.

Johnny nodded yes.

"Do you understand that good sportsmanship is really, really important?" coach asked.

Again, little Johnny nodded yes.

"So," the coach continued, "when you're called out by the umpire, you do not argue or curse at him. Right?"

"Right," replied little Johnny.

"Great," the coach said. "Now go on over there and explain it to your mother!"

Ralph sat Junior down for the 'big talk'. "Soon," Junior's father said, "you're gonna have urges and feelings like you never, ever had. Your hands will sweat and your heart will pound. You're gonna become so fixated you won't be able to think about anything else. Don't worry though, kid. Trust me. It's perfectly normal... it's called golf."

Boxer: Doc, I can't get to sleep at night.
Doctor: Have you tried counting sheep?
Boxer: It doesn't work. Every time I get to nine I stand up.

Long Relief

While Jeff Liefer was a first round draft pick of the White Sox in 1995, his most memorable baseball moment came as a member of the minor league Indianapolis Indians. In 2004, the first basemen went to the bathroom in the clubhouse between innings. He couldn't get out. It wouldn't have been so bad if the Indians simply put in a replacement, but instead, the game was delayed 20 minutes until someone got Liefer out. Of the incident, he remarked, "I don't want to be remembered as the guy who got stuck in the bathroom." Sorry, Jeff.

Jets coach Rex Ryan is so upset over his team's recent losing streak that he decides to visit rival coach Bill Belichick at a New England practice. "Coach, how is it that the Patriots always seem to be on a roll? What's your secret?"

Belichick says, "Watch this." He calls over Tom Brady and says, "Tom, who's your father's brother's nephew?"

Brady responds, "That's easy, Coach...me."

Belichick turns to Ryan and says, That's what it takes, Rex- a smart quarterback. You've got to have a smart QB."

Rex returns to the Jets camp and at their next workout calls over Mark Sanchez. "Sanchez," Rex barks, "Who's your father's brother's nephew?"

Sanchez looks baffled, then asks, "Uh, can I get back to you on that, Coach?"

Annoyed, Ryan says, "Make it quick."

During practice, Sanchez approaches Darrelle Revis and says, "Darrelle, Coach just asked me a strange question: Who's your father's brother's nephew?"

Revis answers, "Duuuh, that's simple. It's me."

Later on, Sanchez catches up with Ryan and says, "Coach, I think I've got it. My father's brother's nephew is Darrelle Revis."

Ryan, exasperated, says, "No, no, no ... It's Tom Brady!"

A golfer walks into the Pro Shop and asks if they sell ball markers. "Yes, says the golf pro, "they're a dollar apiece."

The guy says, "I'll take one," and hands the golf pro a dollar.

The golf pro smiles, opens the register, puts the dollar bill into the tray and then gives the golfer a dime.

QUOTE, UNQUOTE

I don't think there's anybody in this organization not focused on the 49ers... I mean Chargers.".

-Bill Belichick, on his team's preparation

There's Only One Master(s)

Depending on how you look at the situation, Russ Berkman is either a very lucky or very unlucky man…perhaps both. After scoring four tickets to a 2012 practice round at The Masters, Sierra, his Swiss mountain dog, swooped in and devoured them. A panicked Berkman, who had won the tickets in Augusta National's annual lottery, called his girlfriend for advice She told him, "You gotta make the dog puke."

Berkman immediately got to work, putting together a mixture of water and hydrogen peroxide for Sierra to drink. As he explained, "It bubbles in their stomach. It's very safe, and they puke in about 10 minutes."

Sure enough, Sierra did just that. After the four chewed tickets came up in several pieces, Berkman had the unenviable task of putting them back together. After he explained what happened, the folks at Augusta promised to reprint them, thus allowing Berkman to attend the event without his dog's meal ticket.

Then there was the horse that came in so late the jockey was wearing pajamas.

WHAT DO A MUSICAL CONDUCTOR AND A BASEBALL STATISTICIAN HAVE IN COMMON?

The Super Bowl committee has been exploring international possibilities for the event. Among the host sites considered was the new stadium in Warsaw but that was quickly dismissed with the realization that no matter where you sat you'd be behind a Pole.

A guy with a little dog under his arm walks into a sports bar in Cleveland one Sunday afternoon. He sits on a stool and places the dog on a stool beside him. A football game is on the television at the bar. The guy orders a beer and asks the bartender, "What's the score of the Browns game?"

The bartender says, "The Patriots are leading thirteen to nuthin'."

No sooner did the bartender say that than the Browns returned a kickoff for a touchdown. The dog then stood up on the bar stool and started doing somersaults. "Wow! That's really something," says the bartender.

"Oh, he does that every time the Browns score a touchdown," declares the dog's owner. "He's a big Browns fan."

"If he does that for a touchdown, what does he do when the Browns win?"

The guy replies, "I wouldn't know. I've only had him a couple of years."

THEY BOTH KNOW THE SCORE.

Riley says to his psychiatrist, "I'm obsessed with baseball, Doc. It's taken over my life. I eat, drink and think baseball. I even sleep baseball. I dream about it every night. The second I close my eyes I'm running the base paths, fielding a grounder or chasing a fly ball. I wake up more tired than before I went to bed. What can I do, Doc?"

The psychiatrist replies, "The first thing you have to do is to make a conscious effort not to think about the game. For example, when you close your eyes make believe you're watching the lottery results on TV and—wow!—you just won a million dollars!"

"What are you, nuts, Doc?" cries Riley. "I'll miss my turn at bat!"

It's the state prison's championship game. There are two outs in the bottom of the ninth inning. The home team is down by one and the bases are loaded. The catcher walks out to the mound and says to the pitcher, "Take your time. You've got twenty years."

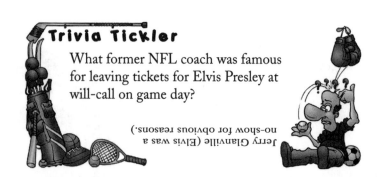

Trivia Tickler

What former NFL coach was famous for leaving tickets for Elvis Presley at will-call on game day?

Jerry Glanville (Elvis was a no-show for obvious reasons.)

The duffer stood over his tee shot. He looked up, then down, up and down, up and down, wiggled around, then looked up and down again until his exasperated partner finally said, "Geez, what's taking you so long?"

"My wife's watching me up there from the clubhouse. I've gotta make a perfect shot."

"Forget about it," his partner said. "You'll never hit her from here."

Pit Stops

A bank robber in Fairview, Pa., who disguised himself with a coat of drywall compound forgot to mask the appearance of the NASCAR-themed Rusty Wallace license plate on his getaway car. Witnesses recognized it and it led ultimately to conviction of the thief.

• • •

At a Chicagoland Speedway qualifying run in 2004, a gigantic inflatable orange promoting race sponsor Tropicana was blown by the wind onto the racing surface, nearly causing Todd Szegedy to wreck when he dodged it.

• • •

A 67-year-old New Jersey man accepted probation, community service and a $1,000 fine after admitting to charges of shooting his family's 20-year-old African Gray parrot with a pellet gun because, as he said, it interrupted his viewing of a televised NASCAR race.

Little Johnny dreamed of going to the zoo and pestered his parents about it day in and day out. Finally his mother nagged his reluctant father into taking Johnny to the zoo for the day.

"So how was it?" his mother asked when they got home.

"Terrific," the father replied. "We had a great time. I was surprised at how much I enjoyed it."

"Is that true, Johnny?" his mom asked. "Did Daddy really have as good a time as you?"

"Yeah, Mom... He sure did- especially when one of the animals came running home at thirty to one!"

A 44-year old man, born on April 4th, has been married for four years, has four kids, earns $44,444.44 a year, and whose lucky number is four, got a racing tip from a buddy. A horse named Four Leaf Clover would be running in the fourth race in the number four spot at the local track that evening. The man hurried to the bank, withdrew $4,444.44, went to the races and bet it all on Four Leaf Clover in the fourth. Naturally, the horse finished fourth.

QUOTE, UNQUOTE

I'm in favor of it.

-John McKay, former Buccaneers coach, when asked about his team's execution after a loss

Boomer's Best

A mainstay at ESPN since the network's inception, Chris Berman is well-known for his catch phrases and the many nicknames he's given athletes. In no particular order, here are twenty of his best.

1. Albert "Winnie The" Pujols
2. Harold "Growing" Baines
3. Moises "Skip to my" Alou
4. Todd "Highway to" Helton
5. Miguel "Tejada they come, Tejada they fall"
6. Mike "You're in good hands with" Alstott
7. Carlos "One if by air, two if" Baerga
8. Scott "Supercalifragilisticexpiali" Brosius
9. C.C. "Splish splash I was taking" Sabathia
10. Todd Which Hand Does He Frohwirth
11. Octavio "Shh" Dotel
12. Lance "You sunk my" Blankenship
13. Bert "Be Home" Blyleven
14. Jon Kitna "Kaboodle"
15. Eric "Sleeping with" Bienemy
16. Bernard "Innocent until proven" Gilkey
17. Darryl Strawberry "Shortcake"
18. Jeff "Brown Paper" Bagwell
19. Mike "Pepperoni" Piazza
20. Joseph "Live and Let" Addai

Q: Where did they put the matador who joined the baseball club?
A: In the bullpen

Calling it a Career

"Quit coaching? I'd croak in a week."
–Bear Bryant, who died of a heart attack a month after retiring

•

"As I walked back to the dugout after striking out, I looked into the stands and saw my wife and kids booing me."
–Fran Healy on how he knew it was time to retire

•

"I didn't make this decision by myself. Thirty teams helped me make it."
–Garret Anderson, former Angels outfielder

•

"Now that I'm retired, I want to say that all defensive linemen are sissies."
–Dan Fouts

•

"When Sandy Koufax retired."
–Willie Stargell, on his greatest thrill in baseball

Two cannibals were scavenging through a garbage can. One of them came across a discarded *Sports Illustrated* swimsuit issue and said to the other, "Look at this menu!"

Biting the Bullet

For those who believe weightlifting doesn't come without risks, consider this. Police in Modesto, California answered an emergency call that found a man with a gunshot wound in his shoulder. It turned out that the unnamed 56-year-old man accidentally shot himself by dropping a dumbbell on a bullet. Officer Chris Adams explained that the man said he dropped the weight on a rimfire .22-caliber bullet and claimed the impact activated its propellant powder. While police didn't find any firearms at the man's home, they did locate a shell casing. The incident now gives a whole new meaning to workout warriors "showing off the guns."

Name Calling

"Chargers" is the team nickname for the new Corner Canyon High School in Draper, Utah, much to the dismay of its students. "Cougars" was their number one choice but it was rejected by the school board on the grounds that it might be offensive to middle-aged women.

Trivia Tickler

Name the two comedians who are in the Baseball Hall of Fame.

Abbott and Costello, for their "Who's on First?" routine

One day on the links, a man was separated from his companions for a few moments and the devil took the opportunity to appear to him. "Say, friend," the devil said in his best used car salesman smile, "how'd you like to make a hole-in-one to impress your buddies?"

"What's the catch?" asked the fellow suspiciously.

"It'll shorten your love life by five years," grinned the devil.

"Hmmm. All right, I'll do it," agreed the man. He then went on to make one of the most spectacular shots ever and aced the hole.

A few minutes later the devil approached the man on the following tee. "How'd you like to go for two in a row?"

"At what cost?" asked the man.

"This'll shorten your love life by ten years."

"You drive a tough bargain, but okay," replied the golfer, who then strode to the tee and sent a 310 yard beauty right into the cup.

At the next tee, the devil appeared once again. "This is a once in a lifetime offer. If you ace this one, it'll be three straight holes-in-one. It's never been done before in the history of the world. But it's gonna cost you another twenty years off your love life."

HOW DO PIGS ROUND THE BASES?

The man proceeded to dazzle everyone by hitting the ball from behind his back, sending it over a huge pond onto the green and right into the hole. It was such an amazing shot that even the devil himself applauded.

And that's the story of how Father O'Malley got into the *Guinness Book of World Records*.

A bunch of chickens were running around a yard when a football flew over the barbed wire fence. One of the roosters clucked, "I'm not complaining, girls, but look at the work they're doing next door."

The psychology professor was giving a lesson on manic depression. He asked the class, "What would you call someone who paces back and forth nervously, screams at the top of his lungs one minute, then sits in a chair sobbing uncontrollably the next?"

A jock from the rear of the class yells out, "I know...a basketball coach."

THEY WENT WEE-WEE-WEE ALL THE WAY HOME.

A Dog and Frys

As Tiger Woods lined up a birdie putt on the 16th green at the 2011 Frys.com Open, Brandon Kelly wound up and threw a hot dog at him. Kelly ran on to the course, yelled out Tiger's name and fired away. He was immediately taken down, arrested and charged with disturbing the peace.

The inspiration for his wacky action: The movie *Drive*, about a stunt driver who moonlights as a getaway driver. Kelly explained, "As soon as the movie ended, I thought to myself, 'I have to do something courageous and epic. I have to throw a hot dog on the green in front of Tiger.'"

The National Hot Dog and Sausage Council did not take too kindly to the event, as Council President Janet Riley released the following statement:

The use of an iconic food in an act of violence against an iconic golfer like Tiger Woods is reprehensible- and a violation of hot dog etiquette. Some might call the thrower a 'wiener,' but we'd say that's too high a compliment. Hot dogs are meant to be enjoyed, not weaponized.

A frustrated golfer, whose ball was lost in the rough, chided his caddie, "Why must you constantly be looking at that pocket watch?"

The caddie responded, "Oh, it's not a pocket watch, sir. It's a compass."

A minister and his very conservative wife had a great marriage except for his long business trips and lifelong obsession with golf. One day while he was away, she was cleaning and found a box of mementos in the back of the bedroom closet. In it she found three golf balls and $800.

Later on when her husband called that night, she asked him the meaning of the three golf balls. He said, "Well dear, I've been keeping that box for twenty years. I'm ashamed to admit it but so great is my passion for the game of golf that I occasionally swear on the course. Every time I use unsavory language, I penalize myself one golf ball."

Shocked that her husband, a man of the cloth, would ever use four-letter words, the wife was at first taken aback but then thought, "Well, three balls means that he's only cursed three times in 20 years. I suppose that isn't so bad."

"All right dear," she said, "I forgive you for your lapses, but tell me, what's the $800 for?"

"Oh that," answered the minister. "I found a guy who buys golf balls at two bucks a dozen."

QUOTE, UNQUOTE

If we were looking for citizenship, we'd disband the league.

-Kevin McHale, when asked how important character is in the NBA Draft

Just for Kicks

It's no secret that plenty of nations around the world are passionate about their soccer. However, fans from Spain's Bilbao made the news in 2012 as a punch line after they set out to see their team play in the Europa League final. They headed to Budapest, Hungary instead of traveling to the correct city-Bucharest, Romania. As soon as they realized their mistake, the fans rushed to get to Bucharest, but were not in time to see their team lose 3-0 to La Liga rival Atletico Madrid. To add insult to idiocy, the stadium announcer greeted the Bucharest crowd by saying, "Good evening, Budapest, and welcome to the Europa League final," which of course set off a chain of boos.

Usain Bolt was about to enter an upscale club when a bouncer stopped him. "You can't come in here wearing jeans," he said.

"Don't you know who I am?" said the world's fastest human.

"Of course I do," replied the bouncer. "And it won't take you long to run home and get changed."

Trivia Tickler

"Fair Hooker, that's a great name, isn't it? But I haven't met one yet." What "dandy" announcer said that when referring to the Browns receiver in the first MNF contest ever?

Dandy Don Meredith, in the Browns 31-21 win over the NY Jets

Grave News

Donald Trump plans to build a cemetery at his Trump National Golf Club in Bedminster, N.J., adjacent to the 5th hole. It'll be the final resting place for The Donald, his family and any of the club's members who wish to be interred there- for an extra fee, no doubt.

• • •

John Henry Smith loved his country and he loved his Steelers. When the 25-year Army veteran died at the age of 55 in 2005, a rather unusual viewing was held for him at a Pittsburgh funeral home. The super fan's body, wearing black and gold silk pajamas- with feet crossed and remote in hand- was laid out in his recliner in front of a TV showing highlights of his favorite football team.

• • •

Major League Baseball licensed a funeral products company, Eternal Image of Farmington Hills, Michigan, to produce team caskets and urns for the die-hard fan.

• • •

The tombstone of William Ambrose Hulbert, who helped found baseball's National League, lies in a cemetery near Wrigley Field and is in the shape of a baseball. Not far from there in a suburban Chicago Jewish graveyard, is a tombstone, which in Yiddish, reads: "The Cubs Stink."

Q: Why did the racehorse sneak behind the tree?
A: To change his jockeys

A guy walks into a sports bar with his German Shepherd. He asks the bartender for a beer. The bartender looks down and says, "I'm sorry, we don't allow dogs here."

The fellow thinks quickly and responds, "He's my seeing-eye dog."

"Oh, I'm sorry," says the bartender. "Here, have one on the house," as he pours the guy a beer. The guy thanks the bartender for the beer, settles down at a table near the door, and begins to watch the football game on the nearest HDTV.

Pretty soon, another guy comes walking in with a small dog. The guy with the German Shepherd whispers, "Psst, buddy. Lemme give you a little tip. They don't allow dogs in here. You gotta tell the bartender that you have a seeing-eye dog."

The other fellow with the pooch thanks him and moseys on up to the bar. "I'll have a draft," he says to the bartender.

The bartender says, "I'm sorry, we don't allow dogs."

The guy answers, "But I'm blind and this is my seeing-eye dog."

The bartender says, "I don't think so. That's a Chihuahua."

The guy says, "What... They gave me a Chihuahua!?!"

QUOTE, UNQUOTE

Just judge people for who they are right now. We're not the Yankees. We're not, thank goodness, the Cubs.

-Mike Krzyzewski, on establishing standards for his Duke Blue Devils

Slapshots

"Hockey players wear numbers because you can't always identify the body with dental records."
-Bob Plager

•

"High sticking, tripping, slashing, spearing, charging, hooking, fighting, unsportsmanlike conduct, interference, roughing... everything else is just figure skating."
-Scotty Bowman

•

"How would you like a job where every time you make a mistake, a big red light goes on and 18,000 people boo?"
-Hall of Fame goalie Jacques Plante

•

"By the age of 18, the average American has witnessed 200,000 acts of violence on television, most of them occurring during Game 1 of the NHL playoff series."
-Sportswriter Steve Rushin

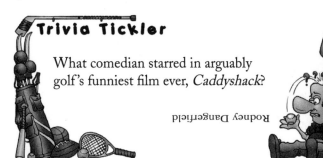

Trivia Tickler

What comedian starred in arguably golf's funniest film ever, *Caddyshack*?

Rodney Dangerfield

"American professional athletes are bilingual; they speak English and profanity."
-Gordie Howe

•

"I went to a fight the other night and a hockey game broke out."
-Rodney Dangerfield

•

"Street hockey is great for kids. It's energetic, competitive, and skilful. And best of all, it keeps them off the street."
-Gus Kyle

•

"We get nose jobs all the time in the NHL, and we don't even have to go to the hospital."
-Brad Park

•

"I was a multi-millionaire from playing hockey. Then I got divorced, and now I'm a millionaire."
-Bobby Hull

HOW MANY CLEVELAND BROWNS DOES IT TAKE TO CHANGE A LIGHT BULB?

A female skier was halfway down the slope when she had to go to the bathroom. With no facilities nearby, she found a sheltered area, dropped her pants and bent down. Suddenly she began to slide backwards, then out into the open and down the slope with her pants around her knees. She crashed and broke her leg.

The woman was rushed to the local hospital by ambulance. When the doctor walked into her room, he was laughing hysterically. He said to her, "You're not gonna believe this, but the fellow in the next room said he fell off a ski lift and broke his arm because he saw a naked lady skiing backwards down the mountain. So, tell me... what happened to you?"

A guy loves betting on the ponies. Every dollar he can beg, borrow or steal is spent at the track. One day his wife becomes very ill and is rushed to the hospital. The inveterate gambler goes to a friend and says, "Please, you've gotta help me. I'm gonna need some money to pay for my wife's hospital bills."

"I'm not loaning you anything, pal," his friend remarks. "You'll just blow it all on the horses."

"Don't be ridiculous," the guy huffs. "Gambling money, I got."

ONE, AND TEN OTHERS
TO RECOVER THE FUMBLE.

Baseball Baffler

Nolan Ryan... Bob Feller... Justin Verlander... Give them their due with their 100 mph heaters, but they couldn't hold a candle to the flame-throwing of Hayden Siddhartha "Sidd" Finch according to *Sports Illustrated's* April 1, 1985, cover story.

The magazine reported that the 28-year-old eccentric rookie from Tibet had been blowing away the Mets coaching staff during spring training with far and away the fastest fastball anyone had ever seen- an amazing 168 miles per hour.

So why was it, then, that Finch's name made an equally quick disappearance from the sports pages?

...Note the date of the issue, April 1- It was an April Fool's joke by the publication.

A man bought four floor seats to an NBA Finals game for he and his three sons. When they arrived at the arena, the man told his kids he had to use the men's room. Meanwhile, the boys me-andered down to their seats only to find a man sprawled out on them.

"Excuse me, sir," said one of the boys timidly, "but I think these are our seats."

"Uuuuuhhhhh," stammered the man.

All three of the boys got scared and ran up the steps. They met their father, who was on his way back from the men's room, and told him what had happened.

The father went down to the seats to confront the man himself. "Excuse me, buddy, but I paid top dollar for these seats. You'll have to leave."

The man remained prostrate on the seats and again responded, "Uuuuuhhhhh!"

At this point, the father decided to complain to an usher, who apologized for the inconvenience and promised to take care of the problem. The usher went down to the seats, approached the man and said, "Excuse me, sir. What's your name?"

"Geee-oooo-rrrr-ggg-e."

"Oh... George, where do you come from? asked the usher.

"Uuuuuupppppppstairs."

A golfing fanatic married a woman whose favorite pastime was attending auctions. Both husband and wife habitually talked in their sleep. One night the golfer yelled, "Fore."

His wife immediately countered, "Four fifty!"

QUOTE, UNQUOTE

Only on days ending in "y".

-Jerry West, when asked how often he'd play golf after retiring from basketball

Two visitors from Greece went to a baseball game. After a few innings, one turned to the other and asked, "Do you have any idea what this is all about?"

The other replied, "No, it's all English to me."

The high school history class was assigned to name who they each considered to be the eleven greatest Americans. As the students were compiling their list, at one point the teacher noticed that little Johnny looked perplexed. "Having a tough time?" the teach asked.

"I've got all but one," answered Johnny. "I just can't decide on the quarterback."

Q: Why was the fighter nicknamed "Rembrandt"?
A: His face was always on the canvas.

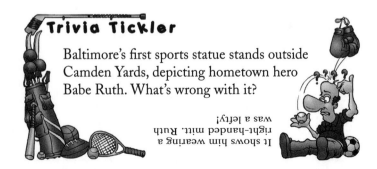

Trivia Tickler

Baltimore's first sports statue stands outside Camden Yards, depicting hometown hero Babe Ruth. What's wrong with it?

It shows him wearing a right-handed mitt. Ruth was a lefty!

Hang it on the Mantle

Mickey Mantle and Billy Martin went on a hunting trip to Mantle's friend's ranch in Texas. Upon their arrival, Mantle went in to greet his buddy while Martin waited in the car.

While inside, The Mick was asked for a favor. His friend had an ancient mule that was ill and going blind. Because the animal had been with him for years, he just could not bring himself to put it out of its misery. Instead, he appointed Mantle the unenviable task.

With Martin outside and unaware of the request, Mantle saw the perfect opportunity to put one over on his Yankee teammate. Pretending to be agitated, Mantle returned to the vehicle, cursing the ranch owner and vowing to get revenge.

Martin, of course, wondered what was the matter. Mantle explained that his "friend" had turned them away and would not let them hunt. "I am so mad at that guy that I'm gonna go out to that barn and shoot one of his mules," he told Martin.

"We can't do that!" Martin exclaimed. Carrying through with his prank, Mantle pushed Martin aside, stormed into the barn and killed the mule.

When he came back out, he saw Martin standing there with a gun, smoke coming from the barrel. "What did you do, Billy?" said Mantle, a panicked look on his face.

"We'll show that son-of-a-bitch," said Martin. "I just killed two of his cows, too!"

"I can't believe my rotten luck," moaned Mulligan. "I haven't had a winning horse in more than two months."

"Hey, maybe you should try out my system," said Hoolihan. "It's worked pretty well for me lately."

"What system is that?" asked Mulligan.

"Well," answered Hoolihan, "it's pretty simple. Every day that I plan on going to the track, that morning I go to church and pray for ten minutes. I've had at least two winners a day since I've been doing that."

Mulligan was ready to try anything so, sure enough, the next morning he went to church and prayed for half an hour. Then it was off to the racetrack. At the end of the day, he ran into Hoolihan. "That system of yours is hooey," Mulligan complained. "I went to church this morning, prayed three times as long as you do and didn't have a single winner all afternoon."

"Where did you go to church?" asked Hoolihan.

"I went to the one on Peach Street," said Mulligan.

"You idiot!" exclaimed Hoolihan. "That church is for trotters."

QUOTE, UNQUOTE

I'm supposed to cut back on dangling participles, and I'm not allowed to split any infinitives for at least another week.

-Vin Scully, legendary baseball broadcaster, after falling at his house and being hospitalized

A Braves fan, Cubs fan, Yankees fan and Red Sox fan went rock climbing one day. All the way up the mountain, they were arguing about who was the most die-hard fan. When they reached the top, the Atlanta fan jumped off the mountain in sacrifice as he yelled proudly, "This is for the Braves...Geronimo-o-o-o!"

Not to be outdone, the Chicago fan committed a "Harry Caray" as he too made the ultimate leap of faithfulness from the mountaintop.

Without a flinch, the staunch Yankee backer shouted, "The curse of the Bambino is back!" and pushed the Red Sox fan off the mountain.

A Couple of Strikes

"True Fact: The Professional Bowlers Association sanctions a tournament called the Odor Eaters Open. It's probably because of all those rented shoes."
–George Carlin

•

"I went to a Chinese bowling alley once. I rented these great shoes, but you weren't allowed to wear them inside."
–Wendy Liebman

Q: How many Charlotte Bobcats does it take the change a flat tire?
A: One, unless it's a blowout...Then the whole team shows up.

Again...We Can't Make This Stuff Up

Danny London, a popular deaf-mute boxer, took a ferocious punch to the head during a fight in New York in 1929. After he regained his senses, he found that he could hear and speak once again. What's more, he won the fight by knockout... Former heavyweight champion Leon Spinks was once mugged. The thugs made off with his money and jewelry- in addition to his two gold front teeth... Gerald Ford, a former All-Big Ten football center, received a toilet seat emblazoned with the University of Michigan seal. Ford liked the seat so much that he reportedly had it installed in the White House while he was President... The New York Giants and Jets jointly owned property in the Meadowlands is called MetLife Stadium but the clubs previously turned down a naming rights offer of $25 million from AshleyMadison.com, on online service for adulterers... When the $23 million Dodger Stadium opened in 1962, there were no drinking fountains...

HOW MANY COLLEGE BASKETBALL PLAYERS DOES IT TAKE TO SCREW IN A LIGHT BULB?

The Milwaukee Brewers held a Bob Wickman poster giveaway night on July 29, 2000. The only problem was that the pitcher had been traded to the Indians the night before the game... Norwegian cross-country skier Odd-Bjoern Hjelmeset's alibi for failing to win a gold medal in the 2010 Winter Olympics: "I think I have seen too much porn in the last 14 days." ... And a German silver medalist in those Games bit off more than he could chew when he broke an incisor after a photographer asked him to bite his medal for a picture. His name- David Moeller.

At the summer Olympic Games, a girl bumped into a guy carrying an eight-foot long stick. "Excuse me," said the girl, "but are you by any chance a pole vaulter?"

"Nein, I'm a German, but how did you know my name is Valter?"

Maybe you've heard about the farmer who crossed his bookie with a hen...He got a chicken that laid odds.

ONE...BUT HE GETS
THREE CREDITS FOR IT.

Mascot Miscues

The Pirate Parrot, mascot of the Pittsburgh Pirates, was once suspended for a game for throwing a Nerf ball at the umpire.

• • •

The San Diego Chicken mascot was sued by the producers of Barney the dinosaur for beating up a look-alike.

• • •

A Missouri resident filed a lawsuit against the Kansas City Royals, alleging that Sluggerrr the Lion hit him in the face with a hot dog, causing a detached retina.

• • •

While attending a game in Tampa Bay, a Boston Bruins fan received an unexpected visit from ThunderBug, the mascot for the Lightning. The fan, who was taunted and sprayed with Silly String, chased after ThunderBug and took him down from behind. The furious man was then escorted out of his seat by security. Shortly after the incident, Kelly Frank, the person inside the ThunderBug costume was relieved of her duties. Upon news of the firing, a "Save Tampa Bay Lightning's ThunderBug's Job" page was set up on Facebook. It quickly received over 1,000 "likes."

Baseball Player #1: How'd you make out with the owner's daughter?

Baseball Player #2: Horrible...no hits, no runs, no heiress.

A college basketball coach scouted a high school player with unbelievable talent. The kid was 7'1" and had great offensive and defensive skills. Unfortunately, his academic skills didn't match. The coach begged the academic dean to admit the kid to the school. Finally, the dean agreed to let the kid in if he could answer three math questions.

The kid was brought in to the dean's office where he was asked the first question. "What's two and two?" asked the dean.

The kid pondered for a few painful moments and finally replied, "Four."

"How much is four and four?"

The kid thought even longer this time before saying, "Eight."

"And now, for your final question, how much is eight and eight?"

The kid paused and paused and paused and then blurted out, "Sixteen."

With that, the coach begged to the dean, "Please! Please! Give him one more chance!"

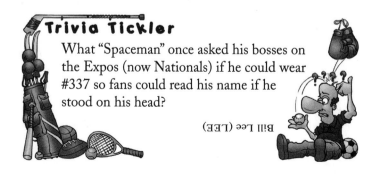

Trivia Tickler

What "Spaceman" once asked his bosses on the Expos (now Nationals) if he could wear #337 so fans could read his name if he stood on his head?

Bill Lee (LEE)

Punch Lines

• Maybe you heard about the Mafioso type who dubbed himself "The Pugilistic Engineer." He made a career of fixing fights.

• Then there was the colorful fighter. He was black and blue all over.

• And, of course, there was the boxing referee who used to work for NASA. Every time a fighter got knocked down, he'd start counting "10, 9, 8..."

• A good fighter always considers the rights of others.

• The toughest thing about fighting is picking up your teeth with your boxing gloves on.

• The fight manager nicknamed his boxer "Laundry" ...Seems he was always hanging over the ropes.

• Did you hear about the fighter who had the misfortune of breaking his nose in two places? He vowed never to go back to either of them.

• And then there was the boxer whose tombstone read, "You can stop counting. I'm not getting up."

• A fighter was in the ring with Siamese twins. After the bout he returned home and his wife asked, "Did you win?" He answered, "Yes and no."

A cricket ambled into a sporting goods store in London. The store's owner, somewhat taken aback to see a cricket with an interest in sports, said, "Hey, we have a popular game that goes by your name!"

"You're kidding," said the cricket. "You have a game called Jiminy?"

Drowning in His Beer

Indianapolis Colts punter Pat McAfee was arrested for public intoxication after taking an early morning swim in a canal. The shirtless McAfee, who was found soaking wet, blamed it on the rain, even though it hadn't rained for days. When police asked him how much he had to drink, McAfee replied, "A lot, cause I'm drunk..."

Q: What do you get when you cross LeBron James and a groundhog?
A: Six more weeks of basketball

Phony Business

According to an Associated Press 2010 article, Cincinnati's
Kroger supermarkets pulled specially designed cereal boxes
featuring former Bengals wide receiver Chad Ochocinco
because of a typo in a phone number for Feed the Children.
The correct number was supposed to be 1-888-HELP-FTC to
assist in supporting the charity, but callers who phoned the
number on the box, 1-800-HELP-FTC, were connected to a
sex line instead.

• • •

Pittsburgh's Troy Polamalu was fined $10,000 by the NFL
for using a cell phone on the Steelers sidelines during a game.
Polumalu had suffered a concussion and simply called his wife
to let her know he was ok.

• • •

Following the death of Apple co-founder Steve Jobs in October
of 2011, Baltimore Ravens offensive lineman Michael Oher
tweeted: "Can somebody help me out? Who was Steve Jobs!"
Oher's tweet came from his iPhone.

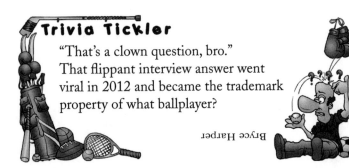

Trivia Tickler

"That's a clown question, bro."
That flippant interview answer went
viral in 2012 and became the trademark
property of what ballplayer?

Bryce Harper

A clerk working part-time in a grocery store was having a difficult time with a customer who kept insisting on buying only half a head of lettuce. Finally, the employee went to his manager and said, "Boss, there's some idiot in the produce department who wants only a half a head of lettuce."

Then, out of the corner of his eye he saw the customer standing directly behind him so he quick-wittedly said, "And this gentleman would like to buy the other half."

After the customer was satisfactorily taken care of, the manager praised the clerk for his quick-thinking and asked, "Where are you from?"

He replied, "From Montreal, the city of hockey players and loose women."

The manager shouted, "Hey, my wife's from Montreal!"

"Which team?" said the clerk.

Bite Me!

Cruiserweight fighter Wali Muhammad was once penalized two points for biting James Salerno. In his defense, he explained, "Why would I bite him? I'm a vegetarian!"

In a pre-fight hype of their 2002 heavyweight championship match, Mike Tyson said to Lennox Lewis, "I want your heart. I want to eat your children." Tyson was forced to eat his words as he lost to Lewis, just as he did to Evander Holyfield when he bit off Holyfield's ear in a 1997 bout.

20/20 Vision

Lindy Chappoten, a pitcher in the class D Sooner State League, was traded by the Shawnee Hawks to the Texarkana Bears of the Big State League. In exchange for the young Cuban hurler, the Hawks received 20 uniforms. It turned out to be a good deal for the Bears. Chappoten went on to win 20 games- one per uniform.

Birthday Suit

Left fielder Carlos May, who played most of his ten-year big league career with the Chicago White Sox, is the only player to wear his birthdate on the back of his uniform. Carlos was born May 17.

The diehard sports fan told his friend, "I've gotta cut down on hot dogs and beer."

"How come?"

"Because I'm starting to get a ballpark figure."

WHAT DID THE ANCIENT ROMANS YELL ON THE GOLF COURSE?

To Be Named Later

Joe Garagiola, a mediocre ballplayer turned broadcaster, commented that "I went through life as a player to be named later."

• • •

Two other players can identify with that- one literally, as in the case of Jose Gonzalez. When he was traded from the St. Louis Cardinals to the San Francisco Giants, Gonzalez decided to take his mother's maiden name and became Jose Uribe.

• • •

Then there's Harry Chiti, a catcher who was traded by the Cleveland Indians to the expansion New York Mets on April 15, 1962 for a player to be named later. June 16, 1962 he became that player to be named later when the Mets sent him back to the Indians; hence, Chiti became the first player ever traded for himself.

The punch drunk fighter was nearly killed in a horse riding mishap. He fell from the horse and was almost trampled to death. Fortunately, the Kmart manager came out and unplugged it.

„i∧I„

Chewing the Fat

"I don't have anywhere to put my elbows when I putt now."
–John Daly, explaining one of the ways his weight loss has been bad for his golf game

•

"Why doesn't the fattest man in the world become a hockey goalie?"
–Comedian Steven Wright

•

"I was going so bad that last week I skipped dinner two days because I was down to .198 and I didn't want anyone saying I wasn't hitting my weight."
–Jesse Barfield, former Blue Jays outfielder

•

"If Howard Cosell had breakfast and dinner with everybody he bragged about on *Monday Night Football*, he'd weigh 723 pounds."
–Joe Garagiola

•

"Obviously, he was a little bit overweight, a little out of shape, but we looked at him and said, overweight and out of shape, he's better than anybody we had last year."
–Tom Wilson, Pistons owner, on acquiring Oliver Miller

After Dallas Cowboys owner Jerry Jones dies and goes to heaven, God is taking him on a tour of the place. He shows Jerry a small three-bedroom home with a tiny Cowboys pennant hanging over the front porch. "This is your eternal home, Jerry," says God. "You should feel mighty proud because most folks don't get their own private living quarters here."

Jerry looks at the home, then does an about face and sees this huge four-story mansion with two gigantic Oakland Raiders flags flying between the four marble pillars. And parked in the circular driveway is a black and silver limo with the Raiders logo on the hood. "Thanks for my home, God," says Jerry, "but I have just one question. You give me this tiny home with a miniature Cowboys pennant and Al Davis gets that beautiful mansion. How come?

God laughs and says, "Oh, that's not Al's home. That's mine."

Q: Why was Cinderella such a lousy football player?
A: Because she had a pumpkin for a coach.

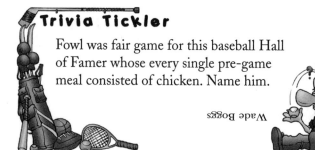

Trivia Tickler

Fowl was fair game for this baseball Hall of Famer whose every single pre-game meal consisted of chicken. Name him.

Wade Boggs

The Disabled List

• In his rookie year, Chicago Bulls guard Derrick Rose needed 10 stitches to close a gash on his arm, which he injured while slicing an apple in bed.

• Valencia midfielder Ever Banegacan was run over by a car- his own. After stopping at a gas station, he forgot to set the handbrake of the vehicle. It rolled backwards, trapping his foot, and causing fractures in his left tibia and fibia bones in his leg.

• Golfer Clay Carpenter suffered severe damage to his leg, stabbed with a broken club shaft in a dispute that began when Carpenter's trio requested to play through ahead of another man's slower foursome.

• Brazilian soccer star Ramalho had to miss several days of action because he was bedridden after taking a suppository orally.

• Norwegian defender Svein Grondalen was training outdoors for an international match during the 1970s when he ran headlong into a moose. He was forced to withdraw from the event.

QUOTE, UNQUOTE

*If everything were going good for him,
he'd be having success.*

-Scott Gordon, Islanders coach,
on the struggles of his goalie, Rick DiPietro

Major League Mishaps

• Joel Zumaya strained his arm playing Guitar Hero and had to sit out multiple games.

• Adam Eaton stabbed himself in the stomach as he was using a knife to open a DVD wrapper.

• Bret Barberie missed a game because he mistakenly rubbed chili juice in his eyes.

• Ken Griffey, Jr. was forced to miss a game after his cup slipped and pinched a testicle.

• Marty Cordova fell asleep in a tanning bed, badly burning himself. He was forced to stay out of direct sunlight, which meant missing several day games.

• After having a nightmare about spiders, Glenallen Hill fell out of bed onto a glass table, receiving cuts over much of his body.

• Jason Bartlett tore the nail off his left pinky while sliding his hand under the television in his room at the Ritz Carlton in Detroit. Juan Castro hurt his neck on the pillow at the very same hotel.

• Steve Sparks dislocated his shoulder trying to tear a phone book in half. He was trying to imitate a group of motivational speakers who had visited the team.

• John Smoltz burned his chest while trying to iron the shirt he was wearing.

A guy desperately wants to go to the Super Bowl, so he goes to a scalper but can get only one ticket. He pays top dollar for a seat in the nose-bleed section, the second to last row of the upper deck.

As the game begins, the guy's watching through his binoculars. He notices that there's an empty seat in the very first row, right on the fifty yard line. As the second quarter is about to end, he looks down and sees that the fifty yard line seat is still empty. At halftime, he makes his way down to the empty seat and asks the guy who's sitting in the next seat, "Is this taken?"

The guy replies, "No."

"Would you mind if I sit here?"

The other guy says, "Not at all. Go right ahead."

"I wonder why someone with a front row, fifty yard line seat wouldn't show up at the Super Bowl," says the first guy.

The second guy says, "Actually, my wife and I have come to every Super Bowl since 1967, but she passed away."

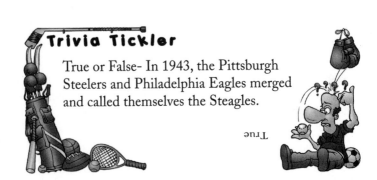

Trivia Tickler

True or False- In 1943, the Pittsburgh Steelers and Philadelphia Eagles merged and called themselves the Steagles.

True

"Oh, gee, I'm sorry to hear that," says the first guy. "But couldn't you get a friend or relative to come to the game?"

"They're all at the funeral."

The Cup Runneth All Over

These days, the Stanley Cup has its own full-time bodyguard, primarily because its past keepers had been known to do some mighty unusual things with it. Way back in 1907, the Montreal Wanderers left it behind after a team photograph, and the photographer's mother made a flowerpot out of it... Once, some Montreal Canadien players left the Cup in a roadside snowbank after they'd fixed a flat tire; fortunately, they later found it where they'd left it... On another occasion, Bryan Trottier of the New York Islanders unscrewed the bowl and used it as a food dish for his pooch... The Cup has even become a sacramental vessel. Tomas Holmstrom of the Detroit Red Wings used it to baptize his baby niece in 2008.

QUOTE, UNQUOTE

This is the only thing that has seen more parties than us.

-**Steven Tyler,** *American Idol* judge and Aerosmith's lead singer, after admiring the Stanley Cup

Doc, I need help," says Mort to the psychiatrist. "It may sound strange, but I keep thinking that I'm a horse."

"I think I can cure you," the psychiatrist answers, "but it's going to take some time and it's going to be extremely expensive."

"Money's not a problem, Doc. I just won the Kentucky Derby."

In the locker room of a golf club, a cell phone sitting on the bench next to Harry started ringing. Harry picked it up and said, "Hello?"

"Darling," cooed a breathy voice at the other end. "I'm on Rodeo Drive and that mink I've had my eye on is on sale- only $25,000."

"Well I guess you should get it then," replied Harry.

"Oh, and while you're on the phone I wanted to ask you- the ashtray in the Ferrari is full. Can I just get a new car?"

Harry shrugged and answered, "Sure."

HOW ARE JUDGES AND BASKETBALL REFS ALIKE?

"And the broker called me about that yacht. He needs to know if I want it. There's $750,000 in the checking account- just enough to cover it."

"Go ahead- live it up," replied Harry.

"Oh, thank you darling. You've been ever so generous," she said as she hung up.

Harry closed the phone, held it up in the air and called out, "Hey- Anyone around here lose a cell phone?"

Potty Permits

Former Marlins manager Jack McKeon told the *Palm Beach Post* that in the early 2000s, he used to make up bathroom passes during games as a way of keeping his players from wandering into the clubhouse. He explained how he handed out "poo-poo cards and pee-pee cards" and "put them where I was sitting (in the dugout), so if you wanted to go to the bathroom you had to get a card. That broke it up."

As the goodwill ambassador to the London Olympics begins to read the opening speech he says, "Oh, oh, oh..." when his aide nudges him and says, "You're reading the Olympic symbol!"

THEY BOTH WORK THE COURTS.

Far From the Norm

First baseman Norm Cash was a five-time All-Star who won the 1961 AL batting title. For the purposes of this book, however, he was a Tigers fan favorite known for his sense of humor. Here are some of Norm's more light-hearted MLB moments:

In 1973, with Nolan Ryan working on his second career no-hitter, Cash was up to bat with two outs in the bottom of the ninth. Teammate Jim Northrup told the popular version of the story: "In his last at-bat, Norm walked up to the plate with a table leg from the locker room. The plate umpire says, 'You can't use that up here.' Cash says, 'Why not, I won't hit him anyway.' He then gets a bat, strikes out on three pitches, and walking away he says to Luciano, 'See, I told ya.'"

•

Once when Cash was caught in a rundown between first and second base, he stopped in his tracks and formed a "T" with his hands to call time-out. It didn't work.

•

On multiple instances when play resumed after a rain delay and Cash had been on base, he attempted to advance himself. For instance, if he was on second before the rain delay, he'd move to third after it.

•

Interestingly, Cash was also noted for never wearing a batting helmet during his playing career. He was one of the few players allowed to do so after helmets were mandated. Perhaps the damage had already been done?

A fellow came home and was greeted at the door by his wife dressed in some very alluring attire. "Tie me up," she cooed, "and do anything you want."

So he tied her up and played golf.

"Coach, coach, I keep seeing spots in front of my eyes?"

"Have you seen a doctor?"

"No, just spots."

A lawyer was reading the will of a wealthy man to members of his family. As he neared the end of it, the lawyer read aloud, "And to my son Waldo, whom I promised to remember in my will even though he played golf all the time and never worked a day in his life...Hi there, Waldo!"

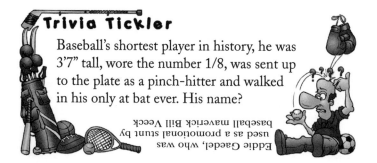

Trivia Tickler

Baseball's shortest player in history, he was 3'7" tall, wore the number 1/8, was sent up to the plate as a pinch-hitter and walked in his only at bat ever. His name?

Eddie Gaedel, who was used as a promotional stunt by baseball maverick Bill Veeck

Hardball Hilarity

Yankees owner George Steinbrenner was infamously known for hiring and firing his managers (Billy Martin no less than five times). In 1982, he promised to change his managerial revolving door policy by saying that "Bob Lemon is going to be our manager all year. You can bet on it. I don't care if we come in last. I swear on my heart he'll be the manager all season." Fourteen games into the season, Steinbrenner dismissed Lemon.

• • •

In a 2002 spring training game, Rockies outfielder Mark Little was hit by a pitch. After going down for a moment, he gathered himself, and proceeded to run to third base.

• • •

On August 29, 1992, Darren Daulton of the Philadelphia Phillies became the 1,000th strikeout victim of Charlie Leibrandt. The Atlanta Braves pitcher decided to keep the ball and rolled it into the dugout for safekeeping. The only problem was that he forgot to call time out and Ricky Jordan, the baserunner on first, cruised into second with what was scored an error.

QUOTE, UNQUOTE

It's not like the selection of women is off the charts here.

-Unnamed Oklahoma City Thunder player

Jim Bouton, former pitcher and author of *Ball Four*, maintains that baseball players are smarter than football players. After all, he says, "How often do you see a baseball team penalized for too many men on the field?"

• • •

At a 1990s minor league contest in Durham between the Bulls and Winston-Salem, a brawl broke out and ten players were ejected. It was "Strike Out Domestic Violence Night".

• • •

Atlanta Braves owner Ted Turner once fell asleep during a 1991 game-- in the tenth inning-- of a World Series game-- the seventh game!

It was Sunday morning and the clergyman should have been at church instead of the bowling alley. He rolled a 300 for his third game, looked up at the heavens and cried, "A perfect game and I can't tell anyone!"

Brief Speech

Pro Football Hall of Famer Paul Hornung got caught with his pants down at a Notre Dame pep rally before a big game against UCLA in 2006. Hornung was at the podium addressing the crowd and was dressed in a sport jacket when his pants suddenly dropped. The former Irish star blamed (or credited) a 47-pound weight-loss to the incident.

Bowling With Barry

You might remember when then candidate Barack Obama bowled a 37 at a Pennsylvania campaign stop in 2008. Very misleading-that was achieved in just seven frames. At that rate, the future U.S. President's score for an entire game would have been a much more respectable 53.

Double Your Pleasure

Q: What do you get if you tie two bikes together?
A: Siamese Schwinns

Q: What did the Siamese twins request at the golf club?
A: Tee for two.

Have you heard about the collegiate football star who's been an undergraduate for eight years?

He can run and tackle with the best of them...but he can't pass.

"Doctor, we've got an emergency! My baby just swallowed all my golf tees!"

"I'll be there at once."

"What should I do 'til you get here, Doc?"

"Practice your putting."

Read All About It

"I bought the book, and it was 175 pages. I put it on the table, and the next morning, it was 225 pages."
–Jay Leno, on Juiced, *Jose Canseco's controversial steroid-filled book*

•

"I thought if I ever got to be famous or great I'd write a book about it. Unfortunately, I couldn't wait any longer. "
–Jim Bouton, Astros pitcher and writer, on the release of his book, Ball Four

•

"I hope the guy sells two million books, because I'll probably buy 100,000 copies and pass them out for free."
–Shaquille O'Neal, on Phil Jackson's book, The Last Season, *which is critical of Kobe Bryant*

•

"Don't bother reading it, kid. Everybody gets killed in the end."
–Peter Gent, telling a rookie not to read the Cowboys' playbook

QUOTE, UNQUOTE

Its a official dat i am leavin skool and enterin draft. ... i aint doin anotha yr.

-Tommy Mason Griffin, Oklahoma point guard, declaring his career choice via Facebook

"No, I was there."
–Yogi Berra, when asked if he'd read his new book

•

"You have to give Pete a lot of credit for what he has accomplished. He never went to college, and the only book he ever read was *The Pe Rose Story.*"
–Karolyn Rose, on her ex-husband

•

"There exists an inverse correlation between the size of a ball and th quality of writing about the sport in which the ball is used. There are superb books about golf, very good books about baseball, not very many good books about football, very few good books about basketball, and there are no good books on beachballs."
-George Plimpton

Q: How does Chad Ochocinco screw in a light bulb?
A: He holds it up in the air and the world revolves around him.

WHAT DO YOU GET WHEN YOU
CROSS AN EVIL WOMAN WITH
A SANDY KOUFAX CURVEBALL

Much Ado About Nothing

In 2003, the Charleston Riverdogs held a "Nobody Night", when no one was allowed in the stadium until after the 5th inning when the game and the attendance- 0 –became official. Fans gathered outside the minor league stadium and rushed in during the 6th inning to collect foul balls that had landed in empty seats during the first five innings.

A Red Sox fan was walking along the beach when a lantern washed ashore. He picked it up and rubbed it. Suddenly a Genie appeared wearing a Derek Jeter jersey. The Genie told the Red Sox fan he had three wishes, but whatever he wished, every single Yankee fan would be granted double that request.

The Boston fan thought long and hard. For his first wish, he asked for a million dollars. Poof! The Sox fan was now a millionaire but, the Genie laughed, every Yankee fan was granted two million dollars. Then the Red Sox fan wished for a brand new Porsche. Poof! The luxury vehicle magically appeared on the beach as the Genie handed him the keys. The Genie snickered as she explained that every Yankee fan now owned two Porsches.

Now it was time for the Sox fan's third wish and he said, "Listen very carefully, Genie. For my final wish, I want you to choke me half to death."

THE WICKED PITCH
OF THE WEST

Insubordinate Clauses

'Twas two nights before Christmas and all through the rink there were 500 fake Santas causing a stink.

It seemed innocent enough. During the height of Christmas season 2003, the New York Islanders offered free tickets to any fan who showed up at their game against the Flyers wearing a Santa suit. But instead of a promotion, all they got was a commotion.

First of all, 500 was more than they expected that night at the Nassau Coliseum- a lot more. The real problem began when the Santas were allowed to parade across the ice between the first and second periods. Now, hockey fans being as they are, a bit of rowdiness was to be expected, but once the Kringles hit the ice it could only be described as mass in-Santa-ty.

The joshing and jostling was good-natured at first but the Santas lost their "puckish" sense of humor when several pseudo St. Nicks ripped off their coats to reveal not bellies that shook like a bowl full of jelly but New York Rangers jerseys. The rivalry between the Islanders and the Rangers is legendary. An NHL Hatfield and McCoy Trick if you will. Relations are icier than the rink they play on.

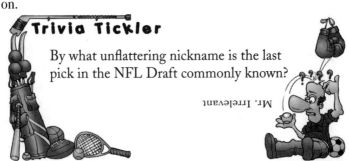

Trivia Tickler

By what unflattering nickname is the last pick in the NFL Draft commonly known?

Mr. Irrelevant

The sight of these Ranger jerseys had the effect of waving red flags in front of hundreds of beered-up bulls and all H-E- Double Hockeysticks broke out.

With the public address system blaring "All Santas will be escorted from the building!" the Santas proceeded to ring each other's bells. The brawl left some Santas with noses redder than Rudolph's but miraculously there were no serious injuries.

As he was dragged out of sight, one Santa supposedly exclaimed, "Merry Christmas to all- it was a helluva fight."

A priest, a doctor and a lawyer were becoming frustrated with the slow play of the foursome ahead of them. "What's with these guys," the lawyer grumbled. "We've been waiting to tee off at least 15 minutes."

"Here comes the greenskeeper," said the priest. "Let's have a word with him."

When confronted, the greenskeeper advised them that the slow-playing group were firefighters and that, sadly, they all lost their sight while saving the clubhouse from a fire a year ago. In gratitude, the club allowed them to play for free anytime.

The priest expressed his concern and said he'd keep them in his prayers, while the doctor volunteered to contact an ophthalmologist buddy to see if there was anything he could do for them.

The lawyer said, "Why can't these guys play at night?"

Headers

"Soccer is not a sport because you can't use your arms. Anything where you can't use your arms can't be a sport. Tap dancing isn't a sport. I rest my case." -George Carlin

• • •

In 2011, Aaron Eccleston, an amateur soccer player in Australia, was ejected from a match after refs found him in breach of uniform rules for wearing an "intimate body piercing." The infraction was uncovered when a ball struck Eccleston in the groin and he fell in agony to the ground, then pulled down his shorts to check for damage.

• • •

Somalia, a midfielder for the Brazilian soccer club Botafogo, was charged with falsely reporting a crime to Rio de Janeiro police after he made up a story about being kidnapped when he was actually trying to avoid a fine for being late to practice.

• • •

Aurel Rusu, the president of a Romanian soccer team, was so dismayed by his team's dismal play that he appointed his son Lucian as the new manager in 1997. Lucian was six months old at the time.

• • •

A player on the English soccer club Chorlton Villa received a yellow card and was booked for "ungentlemanly conduct" in 2009 for breaking wind as an opponent took a penalty kick.

Gremio, a top-flight Brazilian league soccer team, is giving its players Viagra to help improve their circulation when they play at high altitudes.

● ● ●

Manuel Almunia, a goalkeeper for English soccer club Arsenal, was excused from practice to rush home to his wife, who proclaimed she had seen a ghost.

Boulderdash University decides to field a rowing team. Alas, inexperience breeds defeat and they lose race after race. Tired of being the league's doormat, B.U. sends team captain Chuckie Limburger to spy on Harvard, the perennial powerhouse.

Chuckie hides in the bushes along the Charles River in Cambridge and watches the Harvard team practice for a week. When he returns to B.U., he announces to his teammates that he's figured out their secret. "What is it?" one of them shouts out.

"We should have only one guy yelling. The other eight should row."

Then there was the pro football bruiser who was offered seven figures to pen his autobiography. A year later, he turned in the story of his Jeep.

A guy goes to confession. He says, "Father, forgive me, for I have sinned. I was skiing when I saw my boss on the same slope. He didn't recognize me because I was wearing my ski mask so I skied over to where he was, pushed him and roared with laughter as he rolled over and over down the hill."

"Why are you telling me this again?" asks the priest. "That's the fifth time you've confessed this transgression."

The guy answers, "I know. I just like talking about it."

Knock Yourself Out

Boxer Daniel Caruso was getting psyched for a 1992 Golden Gloves bout in New York, pounding his gloves into his face just before the bell rang. He accidentally rang his own bell. Caruso punched himself in the nose, bloodying and breaking it. Doctors stopped the bout before it began.

Q: Why does Jim Kelly eat his Cheerios from a plate?
A: Because he lost all four of his bowls.

QUOTE, UNQUOTE

*I really don't like talking about money.
All I can say is that the Good Lord
must have wanted me to have it.*

-Larry Bird

Not So Fancy Footwork

It was a crucial December 2001 contest between the Arizona Cardinals and New York Giants. Well, not real crucial. But it was a tense moment in the game. Well, not really. It was during the first quarter- but it was a wildly celebratory moment for Bill Gramatica, as every successful field goal was for the Cardinals placekicker. After his kick gave Arizona a 3-0 lead, Gramatica jumped jubilantly up and down, landed awkwardly, tore his ACL and missed the rest of the season.

To this day, the kicker says he's fine with being remembered for something so ridiculous, just as long as everyone knows it wasn't the jump that caused the injury. Tongue planted firmly in cheek, Gramatica said, "My jump was excellent. It was my landing I needed to work on."

A drunk staggered into a local gym where he saw a fighter shadow-boxing in the middle of the ring. A few seconds after watching the boxer dance and punch the air, the drunk called out to the fighter, "Hey! You might as well quit fightin'. The other guy's gone!"

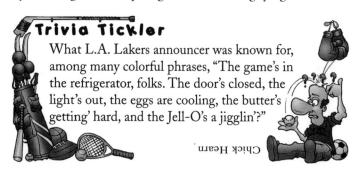

Trivia Tickler

What L.A. Lakers announcer was known for, among many colorful phrases, "The game's in the refrigerator, folks. The door's closed, the light's out, the eggs are cooling, the butter's getting' hard, and the Jell-O's a jigglin'?"

Chick Hearn

Marathon Man

In 1980, Rosie Ruiz was stripped of her Boston Marathon victory after it was revealed she did not run the entire race. Perhaps her inspiration came from the lesser known story of a man in the early 20th century.

Fred Lorz was a professional bricklayer who wasn't much of a runner. That fact didn't change much after the 1904 Olympic Marathon, even though he "won" the race. Lorz took part in the event and actually managed to run the first nine miles. However, that was all he could muster. Totally exhausted, Lorz got into a car driven by his manager. Eleven miles later, he felt ready enough to run the final few miles of the race, winning easily.

When Lorz finally confessed, he was banned for a year from competitive running. And what a difference a year makes...Lorz won the 1905 Boston Marathon, this time all on foot.

The Cleveland Browns have a brand new cologne on the market. It has a slightly different twist. You wear it and the other guy scores.

WHY DID THE UMP THROW THE CHICKEN OUT OF THE GAME?

Keeping Score

At a 1998 Pistons home game, Detroit's Joe Dumars hit a routine free throw. However, after overhearing a Pistons official make a sarcastic remark, referee Joey Crawford thought it was a milestone bucket. He ran over to the scorer's table to tell the P.A. announcer that Dumars had just scored his 20,000th career point. Before anyone could stop him, an announcement was made and Dumars received a standing ovation. "Next time he scores," Crawford later joked, "announce that he just broke Kareem Abdul-Jabbar's (all-time scoring) record."

By the way, Dumars never did come close to the 20,000 mark.

Rerun Regrets

24-year-old Bryan Allison suffered multiple injuries in 2001 when he fell to the ground while throwing a 25-inch TV set off the second-floor porch of his home in Niagara Falls, N.Y., after watching a video of a 1989 hockey playoff game. He and his brother tossed the TV when they became upset over the outcome, which was presumably the same result as twelve years earlier.

Q: Why do the Rams play in a dome?
A: Because even God can't stand to watch.

HE SUSPECTED FOWL PLAY.

Betting Men

September 11, 2010 marked the 25th anniversary of Pete Rose breaking Ty Cobb's all-time record for hits. However, the Reds, who received clearance to honor Rose despite his lifetime baseball ban for betting, had to move the celebration to a day later. Why? Rose was making an appearance at an Indiana casino.

• • •

The NFL suspended Detroit Lions defensive tackle Alex Karras for one year in 1963 for gambling. A couple of years later he was named co-captain of his team. His very first act in his first game as the leader of the team was to participate in the coin toss at midfield. The ref said, "Captain Karras, I will toss the coin and while it's in the air, would you please call it heads or tails."

Karras gently replied, "I'm sorry, sir, but I can't. I'm not permitted to gamble."

• • •

In 1969, first-year head coach Lee Corso manned a Louisville squad that was a heavy underdog against Tulsa. Corso, however, had a plan for the Thanksgiving contest. He put a turkey on a leash to serve as the team's mascot. But the plan was not that simple.

Corso made a bet with the Tulsa coaches that if Louisville lost, they would get to eat the new mascot. Clinging to a late-game lead, Corso called a timeout to remind his defense of the life that was at stake. After they held the lead and won, both Corso and the bird were carried off the field.

A golf club walks into a bar. The bartender says, "Sorry, I can't serve you."

The golf club says, "Why?"

"Because you're going to be driving."

An angry homeowner says to a kid, "Have you seen who broke my window?"

The kid replies, "No but have you seen my baseball?"

School Spirit

Harvey Updyke is an Alabama fanatic who named his children Bear Bryant and Crimson Tyde. In arguably an even more extreme act, Updyke was accused of poisoning century-old oak trees belonging to rival Auburn. While he didn't totally fess up, Updyke did call in to a local radio station and say, "I'm extremely sorry for what I've been accused of doing."

QUOTE, UNQUOTE

What's the difference between a three-week-old puppy and a sportswriter?
In six weeks, the puppy stops whining.

-Mike Ditka

Order in the Sports!

Yogi Berra has caught a lot of pitches in his day but he felt the transit system ads during *Sex And The City* on TBS were foul. One spot presented the multiple-choice question "What is a Yogasm?" The three possible answers were:

1: A type of yo-yo
2: Sex with Yogi Berra
3: What Samantha has with a guy from her yoga class.

Yogi found the commercial "hurtful" and sued for $10 million. But as Yogi himself has said, "It ain't over till it's over," and all parties involved eventually reached an undisclosed settlement. But you can bet that since Yogi was suing the transit system, he probably accepted a "token" payment.

• • •

When Lindsay Lohan saw the 2010 Super Bowl E-Trade Talking Baby commercial in which another baby character is referred to as "that milkaholic Lindsay", it soured her enough to file a $100,000,000 lawsuit alleging that the ad was subliminally about her.

Trivia Tickler

What's golf slang for scoring an 8 on a single hole?

A Dolly Parton

Some thought that she was being a cry-baby while others just thought that she was milking it for all it was worth. In the end though, Lindsay withdrew her lawsuit, E-Trade got millions of dollars more publicity than it paid for and the rest of us were left "udderly" bewildered at the nonsense of it all.

• • •

In 1991, a man sued Budweiser, makers of Bud Light, for $10,000 claiming that contrary to their commercials, his fantasies of beautiful, alluring women lounging around romantic tropical settings did not come to life when he drank their product. In fact, he claimed that this caused him to drink more and more beer, causing him emotional distress and financial loss.

Of course once the case came to a head, a sober judge dismissed it. But not to worry, the man no doubt had several more cases at home.

• • •

Allen Ray Heckard was always being mistaken for Michael Jordan despite being six inches shorter, thirty pounds lighter and eight years older. He could have made it pay off by going to one of those celebrity look-a-like modeling agencies or gotten a job as Michael's personal mini-me but no, he was tired of the whole thing. Michael Jordan may have been one of the all-time greats on the courts but Heckard decided to take him on in the courts.

Heckard sued Michael Jordan along with Nike founder Phil Knight for $832 million in compensation for a laundry list of woes including public harassment, loss of peace of mind, and emotional distress.

According to Heckard, Nike made Jordan even more famous with its ubiquitous Air Jordan commercials, causing him still more distress and so he decided to put on a full court press.

Heckard eventually dropped the suit as it was suggested that he came to the realization that if he lost the case, he'd be responsible for Jordan and Knight's court costs. But who knows? Perhaps if Heckard ever catches Jordan's Hanes underwear commercials, we'll see some more legal "briefs".

Dancer-Duffer Disaster

In 1996, Scott Browning of Houston, Texas, suffered a ruptured achilles tendon at a men's club sponsored golf tournament and was awarded $16,500 in damages. Browning was injured when an exotic dancer who was assigned to be his "designated caddie" and cart driver got so tipsy she overturned their cart into a drainage canal.

QUOTE, UNQUOTE

It could permanently hurt a batter for a long time.

-Pete Rose, on the brushback pitch

EXTRA POINTS

*"I want to be the fastest woman in the world...
in a manner of speaking."*
-Racecar driver Shirley Muldowney

— • —

"Therapy can be a good thing. It can be therapeutic."
-Alex Rodriguez

— • —

*"When I was a kid in Houston, we were so poor we couldn't
afford the two letters, so we called ourselves po'."*
-George Foreman

— • —

*"I used to play sports. Then I realized you can buy trophies.
Now I'm good at everything."*
-Demetri Martin

— • —

*"If one synchronized swimmer drowns,
do all the rest have to drown too?"*
-Steven Wright

"I knew it was going to be a long season when, on Opening Day during the national anthem, one of my players turns to me and says, 'Every time I hear that song, I have a bad game.'"
-Manager Jim Leyland

— • —

"We're not attempting to circumcise rules."
-Pittsburgh Steelers coach Bill Cowher

— • —

"Once when I was golfing in Georgia, I hooked the ball into the swamp. I went in after it and found an alligator wearing a shirt with a picture of a little golfer on it."
-Buddy Hackett

— • —

"I pulled a hamstring during the New York City Marathon. An hour into the race I jumped off the couch."
-David Letterman

WHAT DO YOU CALL A SEATTLE SEAHAWK WEARING A SUPER BOWL RING?

"If you are caught on a golf course during a storm and are afraid of lightning, hold up a 1-iron. Not even God can hit a 1-iron."
-Hall of Fame golfer Lee Trevino

— • —

"That silver medal at the Olympics, that's something, isn't it? You get gold, you've won. You get bronze, 'Well, at least I got something.' But silver is basically saying, 'Of everyone that lost, you were the best. No one lost ahead of you; you are the very best loser.'"
-Jerry Seinfeld

— • —

I had this great idea to make the Great Wall of China a handball court."
-George Gobel

— • —

"A guy from Kenya won the Boston Marathon. In fact, only one American finished in the top ten, and he was driving an SUV."
-Jay Leno

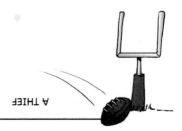

A THIEF

*"No game that can be played by a person with a wad
of tobacco in his mouth is a sport."*
-Andy Rooney

— • —

*"The one drawback, of course, is that it
looks a lot better than it performs. "*
**-Michael Ventre, of msnbc.com,
on Anna Kournikova's "Anna Bra"**

— • —

*"Fear was absolutely necessary.
Without it, I would have been scared to death."*
-Floyd Patterson, former heavyweight champ

— • —

*"Players sometimes benefit from a change of scenery.
Well, good players can benefit from a change of scenery.
Bad players are bad players wherever they are."*

-Doug Moe, NBA coach

— • —

*"There is a great excitement when you have a legit chance
to get that carrot at the end of the rainbow."*

-Charles Barkley, on the NBA's 2009 Opening Night